Source Books in
Landscape Architecture

Michael
Van Valkenburgh
Associates

1 Allegheny Riverfront Park

Jane Amidon, Series Editor

D1245149

Princeton Architectural Press, New York

Published by
Princeton Architectural Press
37 East Seventh Street
New York, New York 10003

For a free catalog of books, call 1.800.722.6657.
Visit our web site at www.papress.com.

The seminars and publications for this series are made possible
by the generous support of DeeDee (BSLA 1988, Knowlton
School of Architecture) and Herb Glimcher.

Editing and layout: Megan Carey
Design: Jan Haux

Special thanks to: Nettie Aljian, Dorothy Ball, Nicola
Bednarek, Janet Behning, Penny (Yuen Pik) Chu, Russell
Fernandez, Clare Jacobson, John King, Mark Lamster, Nancy
Eklund Later, Linda Lee, Katharine Myers, Lauren Nelson,
Molly Rouzie, Jane Sheinman, Scott Tennent, Jennifer
Thompson, Paul G. Wagner, Joseph Weston, and Deb Wood
of Princeton Architectural Press —Kevin C. Lippert, publisher

Library of Congress Cataloging-in-Publication Data

Michael Van Valkenburgh : Allegheny Riverfront Park /
compiled and edited by Jane Amidon.
     p.   cm.   — (Source books in landscape architecture)
   Includes bibliographical references.
   ISBN 1-56898-504-5 (pbk. : alk. paper)
  1. Van Valkenburgh, Michael—Interviews. 2. Landscape
architects—United States—Interviews. 3. Landscape
architecture—United States. 4. Allegheny Riverfront Park
(Pittsburgh, Pa.) I. Amidon, Jane. II. Series.
   SB470.V34M53 2005
   712'.092—dc22
                                                      2005003475

Contents

Acknowledgments

A depth of appreciation is due first and foremost to Michael Van Valkenburgh for participating with wit and wisdom in the inaugural Glimcher Distinguished Visiting Professorship seminar. With customary insight that provoked students to strengthen their understanding of built landscapes, Michael set the bar high for all involved. The honesty of opinion and design leadership that impressed us as graduate students in the early 1990s continue to be hallmarks of Michael's impact on contemporary landscape architecture.

We are fortunate to have a project such as the Allegheny Riverfront Park to serve not just as the subject of the first Source Book in Landscape Architecture but as an inspiring model for urban park-making today. Many thanks to the combined talents of Michael Van Valkenburgh, Laura Solano, and Matthew Urbanski of Michael Van Valkenburgh Associates (MVVA), artists Ann Hamilton and Michael Mercil, and Carol Brown of the Pittsburgh Cultural Trust.

A roundtable discussion on the Allegheny Riverfront Park was held at the Knowlton School of Architecture in 2002. Threads of discussion opened there proved important to this publication. In addition to the design team named above, I am grateful for the commentaries of the invited critics Ethan Carr, Erik de Jong, and Gary Hilderbrand (whose comments and essay, respectively, appear in this book). Thanks also to the students who participated in the seminar: Jeff Anderson, Eric Brightman, Jennifer Caputa, Lin Goepfert, Tim Hess, Indy Idvakil, Kris Lucius, Anne McKisson, Gabriela Patocchi, Adam Ravestein, and especially Jason Brabbs for videography and Jill McKain and Cheryl Somerfeldt for written contributions.

These books would not be possible without the support of many at the Knowlton School of Architecture and the generous patronage of the Glimchers. The encouragement of Robert Livesey is essential to the program. Advice offered by Jeff Kipnis and Todd Gannon was helpful in producing the first Source Book in Landscape Architecture. At MVVA, Jane Glazier, Jason Siebenmorgen, Gullivar Shepard, and Matt McMahon were instrumental in the book's production. Finally, the editorial guidance of Megan Carey and Kevin Lippert at Princeton Architectural Press is much appreciated.

Source Books in Landscape Architecture

Today there is a hunger for transparency. Source Books in Landscape Architecture provide concise investigations into contemporary designed landscapes by looking behind the curtain and beyond the script to trace intentionality and results. One goal is to offer unvarnished stories of place-making. A second goal is to catch emerging and established designers as facets of their process mature from tentative trial into definitive technique.

Each Source Book presents one project or group of related works that are significant to the practice and study of landscape architecture today. It is our hope that readers gain a sense of the project from start to finish, including crucial early concepts that persist into built form as well as the ideas and methods that are shed along the way. Design process, site dynamics, materials research, and team roles are explored in dialogue format and documented in photographs, drawings, diagrams, conceptual sketches, and models. Each Source Book is introduced with a project data and chronology section and concludes with an essay by an invited critic.

This series parallels the Source Books in Architecture as conceived by Jeffrey Kipnis and Robert Livesey at the Austin E. Knowlton School of Architecture and is a synthesis of the Glimcher Distinguished Visiting Professorship. Structured as a series of discussion-based seminars to promote critical inquiry into contemporary designed landscapes, the Glimcher program gives students direct, sustained access to leading voices in the profession. Students who participate in the seminars play an instrumental role in contributing to discussions, transcribing recorded material, and editing content for the Source Books. The seminars and Source Books are made possible by a fund established by DeeDee and Herb Glimcher. Together they and their family are patrons of the arts and social service organizations.

Preface

Carol Brown

Industrial Pittsburgh has long been noted for the quality of its architecture, beginning with Henry Hobson Richardson's courthouse and jail designed and constructed in the 1880s. For more than one hundred years, however, the city failed to acknowledge the natural beauty of its river setting. Despite such efforts as the Olmsted brothers' 1910 proposal for a riverfront park system beginning at "the Point" where the Monongahela and Allegheny rivers join to form the Ohio, and the eventual construction of Point State Park at that confluence in the 1950s, Pittsburgh's riverbanks became long corridors of highway separating the city and its people from the pleasures of its rivers.

In 1984 the Pittsburgh Cultural Trust was formed to create a cultural district in a neglected fourteen-square block of downtown edged on one side by the Allegheny River. Initial planning for the district called for holistic development focusing on the creation of arts and entertainment venues and enhancement of the district's built and natural environment, including historic loft buildings, public art, open space, streetscapes, and the Allegheny Riverfront.

With district planning completed in 1994, the Cultural Trust turned its attention to the river. The Trust issued a request for qualified teams of landscape architects and artists to design the Allegheny Riverfront Park. Unanimously selected from an international field, Michael Van Valkenburgh Associates (MVVA), with Ann Hamilton and Michael Mercil, created a stunning, award-winning park.

The challenges of the site became the strengths of the final design of the park. Two parallel linear spaces dissected by highways, with vastly different elevations and periodic flooding, led MVVA, Hamilton, and Mercil to create an innovative, complex and highly successful design vocabulary for the park. The lower-level pathway along the river's edge, rich with riparian plant materials and native boulders that suggest the natural beauty of a Western Pennsylvania riverbank, connects by way of elegant vine-walled and accessible ramps to an upper level defined by the firmer and more constructed lines of a city, set with bluestone paving, banks of bluestone seating, and more formal plantings.

The park is not only a gift of the river to the people of Pittsburgh, particularly to patrons and residents of the cultural district, but a handsome example for all cities in the challenge of reclaiming more riverbanks in the urban core.

JUNE 1994

The Pittsburgh Cultural Trust issues a call for qualifications for the design of a park along the Allegheny River. Five teams are selected to submit proposals.

SEPTEMBER 1994

The commission is awarded to Michael Van Valkenburgh Associates and Ann Hamilton.

Programming and pre-design research begins.

MVVA team takes boat ride up the Allegheny River and discovers native plants that colonized industrial sites at the river's edge, inspiring the plant palette for the lower-level park.

NOVEMBER 1994

MVVA proposes to cantilever the walk to gain additional space for the lower-level park pathway in response to the public's desire for riverfront access.

MARCH 1995

Design development of the upper- and lower-level parks begins.

APRIL 1995

Construction documents for the lower-level park are completed.

19 JANUARY 1996

Allegheny River floods, reaching near-record levels. Heavy rains combined with snow melt—brought on by temperatures in the sixties—causes major flooding in the entire upper Ohio River basin. The flooding of the Allegheny is compounded by an ice jam that breaks near Parker, PA.

JUNE 1996

Lower-level park construction is delayed by one year due to flood. Park elements are reengineered.

MARCH 1997

The city of Pittsburgh receives an ISTEA grant for the redesign of Fort Dusquesne Boulevard.

JUNE 1997

Construction of the lower-level park begins.

NOVEMBER 1998

Lower-level park is dedicated.

Data and Chronology

ALLEGHENY RIVERFRONT PARK

Pittsburgh, Pennsylvania

CLIENT:

Pittsburgh Cultural Trust

DATA:

Lower-level Park
Park length: 3,700'
Average width: 31'
Grade change at ramps: 17'-6"
Length of ramps: 352' each
583 trees
1,480 boulders

Upper-level Park
Park length: 1,920'
Average width: 32.5'
147 trees
3.4 tons of bluestone
62,000 cubic yards manufactured soil

MARCH 2000
Construction documents issued for upper-level park bid.

JULY 2000
Construction begins on upper-level park.

MAY 2001
Upper-level park is dedicated.

4 JULY 1999
The annual Three Rivers Regatta takes advantage of the new riverfront park for the Fourth of July celebration.

JUNE 2001
MVVA presents proposal for the east and west extensions of the Allegheny Riverfront Park.

SEPTEMBER 2004
Flooding of the Allegheny River, caused by the remnants of a rampant hurricane season in the southeastern U.S., completely submerges lower-level park.

Conversations with Michael Van Valkenburgh

Compiled and edited by Jane Amidon

The following exchange took place during the course of six visits made by Michael Van Valkenburgh to the Knowlton School of Architecture as the inaugural Glimcher Distinguished Visiting Professor. Additional comments by members of the design team are taken from a roundtable discussion.

Jane Amidon: **You've mentioned that major aspects of your early career were influenced by several of the leading postwar modernists such as Dan Kiley and Rich Haag. Much of your research at this time focused on the garden scale—appropriate to the 1980s, as many in the profession returned to the idea of critical site design after decades of greater concern with environmental and social issues. Your research, resulting exhibition, and publication of** *Built Landscapes: Gardens of the Northeast* **in 1984 helped support the renewed focus on articulation of site-specific qualities.**

What were you exposed to, and how can we identify thinking that has been carried from this into your current work with parks at the urban scale?

Michael Van Valkenburgh: Ten years out of undergrad, I was concerned that the profession was turning its back on design. The garden was a means to look more closely at design. I had recently signed on as an assistant professor at Harvard and had just worked for four years for Kevin Lynch, the city planner. Kevin had great respect for landscape as a design medium; he believed that if you could create beauty in a small space and solve the programmatic requirements of the garden, you could probably work on landscapes at any scale. I set out to interview garden designers whose work I admired, including James Rose, A. E. Bye, and Dan Kiley (many of whose projects I had visited on a self-guided tour in 1973). Alan Ward sometimes traveled with me to capture the gardens in photographs. I was also interested in Beatrix Jones Farrand, whose work I had studied during a Dumbarton Oaks fellowship. It was important to include her as a non-modern in the show, in addition to Fletcher Steele, who in some ways was a bridge between the great neoclassical estate designers and modern landscape architecture. Most of all, I wanted to visit the gardens with the designers themselves and to have the landscapes properly photographed. I wanted to make the profession look noble, the way it is. I wanted to create a museum-quality exhibition that would make people see landscape architecture as a profession of beauty. Although they intimidated me, I was inspired by discussions with Kiley, Bye, and especially Rose, who gave me a lot to think about. I met these three men at the mature peak of their careers. It convinced me that I loved landscape architecture. It was affirming to share their passion. The show was influential to me; I saw it as a documentary, not an artistic investigation.

In terms of connections between some of my early academic work and my office's current urban parks projects, one could say that Lynch influenced my understanding of the urban condition as it relates to parks. In some ways, the design of a park is not unlike the design of a garden. But the scale is wildly different. And the complexity of context—what's around it—changes a lot. Both provide experiences of color, space, texture, and an immersion within landscape material as an art form. But a garden is for an individual, and a park is for everyone.

There was an important internship in London in 1970 with the English garden designer Dame Sylvia Crowe. Plants are the key to my designs at every scale. If you don't deeply love a Kentucky coffeetree or a forest of bamboo or the way a Kousa dogwood explodes into bloom in June, you probably should get out of landscape architecture.

Built Landscapes: Gardens of the Northeast, 1984.
Exhibition curated by Michael Van Valkenburgh,
photographs by Alan Ward. Garden designers:
TOP LEFT and RIGHT: James Rose and A. E. Bye
BOTTOM LEFT and RIGHT: Dan Kiley and Fletcher Steele

Teardrop Park, Battery Park City, New York, New York, 1999–2004. Model charette and design session at MVVA's New York office

opposite:

TOP: Mill Race Park, Columbus, Indiana, 1989–93
BOTTOM: Tahari Courtyard, Millburn, New Jersey, 2002–03

JA: **What's the typical design process in the office?**

MVV: We consider many ideas; we try to invent new things as often as possible. We build study models—3-D models that can be felt, picked up, and looked at—and we talk a lot about the models. Every project of ours is mostly about its spatiality and its materiality. The models aren't fancy. They are tools that we use to look at space. We don't design in Photoshop and we rarely do big presentation models. At the beginning of a project, a lot of our process goes from rough, small sketches, to models, then into a computerized drawing to dimensionally check things, then back to models. Scale changes and looking at things in section are mixed in.

We sometimes have a problem with new MVVA staff who have worked in other offices and think that there are designers and then others who get it built. We see design as all aspects of the process, and as such, our projects represent a collaboration by everyone in the office. We don't end the design concept when we start the construction documents. Instead, we use the building process to intensify the design, as a way to learn.

JA: **The issue of truth to one's medium is important to you as both a landscape architect and a painter. Why?**

MVV: For landscape architecture to be emancipated from architecture, it must be defined on its own material terms. We still let so many other design sensibilities define what the aesthetics are in landscape architecture, rather than having our own language, our own agreed-upon things that define landscape as a medium. Think about the 1950s when painters such as Jackson Pollock and Joan Mitchell gave up representation and began dealing with the intrinsic qualities of paint—once that occurred and then painters went back to

Drawing by Michael Van Valkenburgh, January 1990

opposite:

LEFT and RIGHT: Spider Island, Chicago Botanic
Garden, Chicago, Illinois, 1999–2000. Installation of
meadow sod

representation, they went back to it in a different way. Painting was forever altered by that abstract exploration. In a way, we are just now reaching that moment in landscape architecture. I don't think we've had our abstract expressionism yet; we haven't had the blues yet, which set musicians free earlier in the twentieth century. This is the exciting thing that is happening right now in landscape architecture.

JA: **What is the medium of landscape architecture? Obviously it includes but is larger than the physical ingredients. Many see the articulation of time and environmental phenomena as the essence of your work. Ten years ago Peter Rowe described your medium as the spatial registration of flux.**

MVV: My work now is less about registering flux and more about welcoming it into my process and design. As such, the exploration of materials is essential—the temporality of vegetation, the water-ness of water. Goethe said, "Art should not simply speak to the mind through the senses, it must also satisfy the senses themselves." The beauty of landscape so often lies within its complexity. Even its form is complex. Design is about ambiguities, contradictions, degrees. I embrace that. I'm not a linear person. Being rational, linear, or analytical is not my emphasis.

I was thinking recently that a landscape is more like a poem than a novel. As with poetry, a landscape requires the reader to want to be a participant, to add the important part of experience to the realization of the piece. That is a different kind of writing—and reading—than a novel. Similarly, architecture is a different kind of construction of space than landscape is; it has a more monolithic, comprehensible quality of a story as opposed to a landscape. In a landscape often you don't know where the boundaries or the edges are…and not knowing that is part of what

you take advantage of if you are a good landscape architect.

I'm interested in folding seasons and phenomenology into my work. I focus on celebrating the material properties of landscape rather than suppressing them. Non-native plants are good; they can be anthropomorphic. I'm more confident these days in using color and experimenting with difficult plants such as sumac and moss. In landscape the medium is alive; you are dealing with something in constant transition. Plantings can be thought of as nature reconceived: *in vitro*, not as a finished aesthetic. I'm interested in the structure of space toward a larger kind of spatiality that includes psychological dimensions. How you open up the doors of people's imaginations has to do with the construction and sequencing of episodes in a landscape and with bold, intentional use of plants and land form. We prefer thick plantings that can be thinned over time as nature does—it's an approach that should not be confused with just

being natural but is something excited, electrified, kinetic. It is the exaggerated presence of nature— *hypernature*—that makes me think of music and painting informed by borrowing and reassembling of material essences.

Recently I was meeting with a group of people from Cincinnati interested in parks. They asked, "What makes a great park?" I answered and they nodded their heads in agreement, but I realized later that my response was inadequate. I said, "Great parks exploit the medium of landscape." They might have thought that I said the equivalent of, "What makes great music is music." I should have gone on to say, "And let me tell you what some of those particular things about landscape are: it is a unique vehicle for prying open what Bachelard calls our psychological intimate immensity, the *Being John Malkovich* part of who we all are." Landscape lets people go into incredibly wonderful places—secret gardens—in their imaginations. The thing that defines landscape as

Garden on Turtle Creek, Dallas, Texas, 1997–99.
Stainless steel stair floats over tree roots and hovers
above new plantings

a medium, connecting it to our imagination, is that it is alive. And there is no other art form that is always moving forward as a living system—it is wonderful. That is why this thread of exaggerated naturalism is so important in my office's work. It introduces that element of chance—a kind of temporality and complexity that comes with something being alive.

JA: **Could regionally oriented plantsmen such as Roberto Burle Marx and Jens Jensen serve as precedents for what you are doing right now versus what you were doing fifteen years ago (designs of explicit structure)? Not knowing your history, one could look at some of your current projects and see parallels in the use of plants, as a contextualizing palette of habit, texture, and growth pattern.**

MVV: I like that idea and hope it is true....I have only seen one tiny Burle Marx project in person,

but even with this handicap, I'm a great admirer of his work. I started in this direction you describe as a result of my conversations with James Rose in the early 1980s. Rose made me realize that the materiality of plants is plenty to chew on, and A. E. Bye's complex "wild" gardens gave me more satisfying beauty than I expected. He somehow gave me permission to let a love of naturalism slip into my work.

JA: **Naturalism raises the question of subtlety. Do you worry about it? In the projects you've shown us, we see the trajectory move from highly ordered compositions in the 1980s, such as 50 Avenue Montaigne and the Eudoxia scheme, to late-1990s plant massing as process-based sculptural form, such as the maples at the New School or the prairie meadow at General Mills Headquarters. Today we see intentional plays on dissolution of order, such as at Harvard Yard, and nearly impressionistic**

Garden on Turtle Creek. Fountain as retaining wall

Vera List Courtyard, New School University, New York, New York, 1990–97, with artist Martin Puryear

opposite:

TOP: Teardrop Park, Battery Park City, New York, New York, 1999–2004, with artists Ann Hamilton and Michael Mercil

BOTTOM: Teardrop Park. Icewall

sublimation of site structure. We find blatant revelations of horticultural, geological, and topographical qualities in the recently completed Teardrop Park in Manhattan. In fact, in describing Teardrop Park you speak of "empowering" the designed, urban landscape by restoring, even reconstructing, a piece of the long-gone escarpment. Three thousand tons of rock were trucked in; a limestone face has rivulets of water that "recall wild streams of upstate New York." Do I hear echoes of Frederick Law Olmsted and thunders of the picturesque?

MVV: If you hear thunders of the picturesque, then that thunder is far away, and after Teardrop Park, likely not to get any closer! These themes are more appealing to the everyday guy and therefore relevant, if not essential, in American parks. Who are we designing parks for—the people who talk about landscape or the people who actually use it? You could say that my office designs for a

signature ambiance, or feeling, over a signature style. Sometimes it's taking nature and organizing it. We try to create landscapes with a depth of experiences that alter people's feelings rather than superficially entertain them. A landscape should hold you, temporarily remove you, to be legitimate. You know where you are and where you aren't; orientation inward is not disorientation. Parks, especially in the city, should be about imagination and experience.

If we ever replicate nature, it's with a twinkle in our eye. For example, at the General Mills Headquarters, you have a classic 1950s Skidmore, Owings and Merrill building forty feet away and two lanes of traffic all around. I see what our office did with the prairie fragment as not copying nature but rather borrowing pieces. When we use something natural in our design, it is a strategy, it is a collage of parts.

The most important thing about a park is that it is a place of consummate freedom within

Entry landscape, General Mills Corporate
Headquarters, Minneapolis, Minnesota, 1989–91.
Controlled burning of field occurred annually to
maintain native prairie species.

opposite:
Entry landscape, General Mills Corporate
Headquarters, with sculpture by Mel Kendrick.
Destroyed in 1999, the design was replaced with a
"mow, blow, and go" landscape.

Lake Whitney Water Treatment Plant landscape, New
Haven, Connecticut, 2001–05. Site design and
landscape by MVVA; building by Steven Holl Architects

Reinvigoration of Alumnae Valley, Wellesley College, Wellesley, Massachusetts, 2001–05 (work in progress). Designed wetland will filter particulates, absorb nutrients, and lower temperature before releasing the treated water into Lake Waban.

a city. Pieces of nature help facilitate the dreaming, the imagining that we all want in parks. That's part of what a great park must provide.

I used to be troubled about liking Olmsted, but now I have a great love for his work. Robert Smithson held him in the greatest regard. Olmsted understood so much about the medium of landscape, its expressive and experiential power to connect to place and context. Landscape architects spend too much time worrying about "real nature" versus "constructed nature" when both are alive and are part of the same ecological essence. There are more important issues facing us today.

JA: In *Built Landscapes*, you wrote that the idea of the park is timeless and universal, that "the very word conjures in our minds a place to escape from a harassed life, an environment for relaxation, respite from stress, a change of scene. The scene does not have to be a tranquil one. It can be one that is grotesque or harsh or sublime. People will enjoy the change." Given this definition, one might believe that the dialectic of nature and culture has not changed significantly since the Industrial Revolution. How do you reconcile this stance with a number of recent park proposals and competitions that deal with the metropolis as an extended horizontal condition, that offer a systems-based matrix to signal a shift from the pictorial to the operational? Do they run the risk of creating an indexed nature bank versus a rooted place, and at what point does open-endedness conflict with truly resilient, constructed nature?

MVV: Indexed and operational? Landscape is so much more important and wonderful than that. These ideas are fleetingly interesting in the realm of "different," but not worthy of a long look. It's sad to think that the word "park" might not have something to do with experiential anticipation.

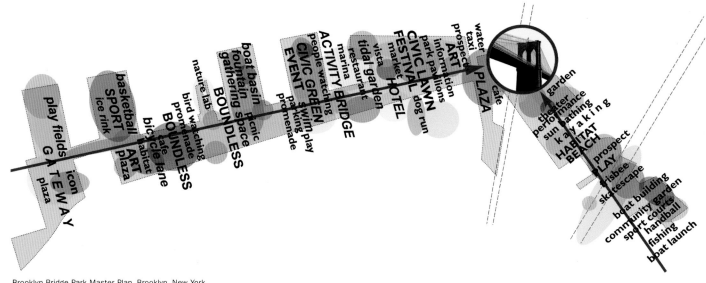

Brooklyn Bridge Park Master Plan, Brooklyn, New York,
2004

Parks are about the meaning of democratic society, not an easy thing to put in a museum exhibition. It sounds grand that people will colonize the site and provide the program, but how? Why? People and societies are more complex than that. Olmsted was correct when he said a great park must have "range." Parks need an accessible aesthetic and a legibility for all to feel welcomed. Park designers should be invisible in a sense, because public landscapes shouldn't be overly about one designer's individual expression. There is a lack of understanding about what it takes to keep a park going once it is built; otherwise it's like buying a puppy but not figuring out who's going to raise it.

If these recent meta-landscape theorists knew the disasters, the extra time, the volunteering, the following up without getting paid that we do when we try to experiment with "reforestation," for example, or with even a grain of the stuff that they are talking about, their ideas would change.

You could write a book of case studies on how complicated it is to make a meadow or a forest in a park. It is an art form and it has a craft. These park proposals you describe are like the equivalent of going to South Carolina, where people have been making baskets for three hundred years, and deciding that you are going to make a basket yourself. And you just draw a shape and you start being expository about shape and you have absolutely no idea about how the basket gets made. But how the basket gets made deeply informs that shape.

What these "indexed and operational" proposals are saying that is good is that the park has been ignored by society so now we need a new way to design parks. I agree with this, and having the discourse take place is the best. But there is a fine tradition of landscape architects playing the lead role in park-making that doesn't need to be diminished by thinking about pseudo-systems that pretend to be superior to the long history of

Brooklyn Bridge Park Master Plan.
Rendering, January 2005

our profession. The park tradition comes out of something important—it comes out of the urban form of cities and democracy needing shared public spaces. I'm glad that people are trying to do new things, but it's just that their ideas feel so silly in their shameless disregard of our own history. I don't find that these proposals honor what is powerful about public landscapes.

Landscape architecture, which values synthetic thinkers, is poised to be in its most important period as a profession. We have the capacity to design things as living and social systems. We're able to think both small and big. We have professional bridges to engineering and to the natural sciences and to art. A lot of our projects over the next ten years will out of necessity come from environmental remediation work. Landscape architects are positioned to lead this work.

Site Plan

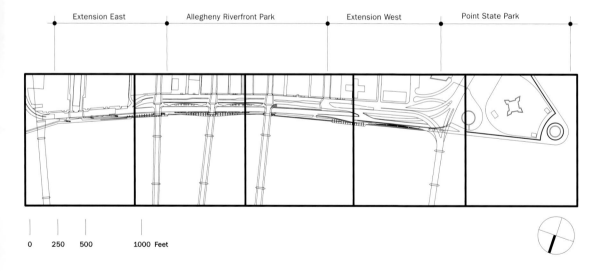

Extension East | Allegheny Riverfront Park | Extension West | Point State Park

0   250   500   1000 Feet

Allegheny Riverfront Park and proposed eastern
and western expansions, Pittsburgh, Pennsylvania,
1994–2001. Site plan key

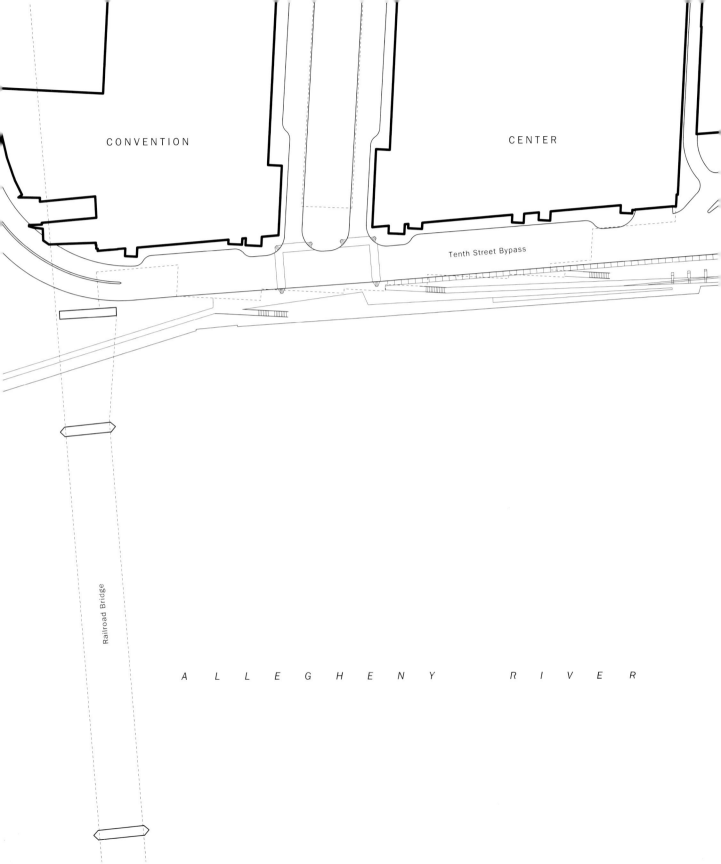

CONVENTION

CENTER

Tenth Street Bypass

Railroad Bridge

A L L E G H E N Y   R I V E R

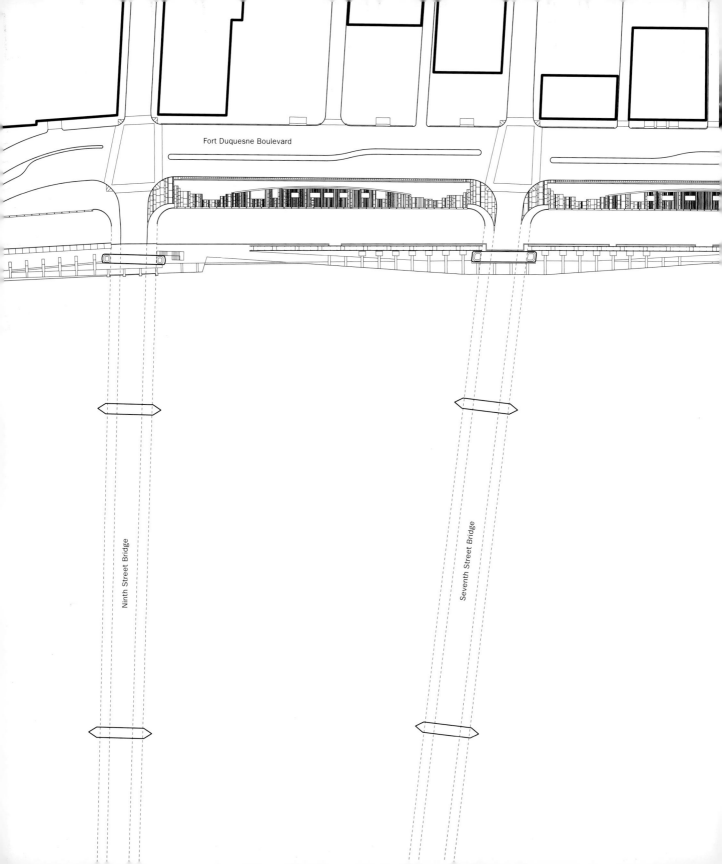

Fort Duquesne Boulevard

Ninth Street Bridge

Seventh Street Bridge

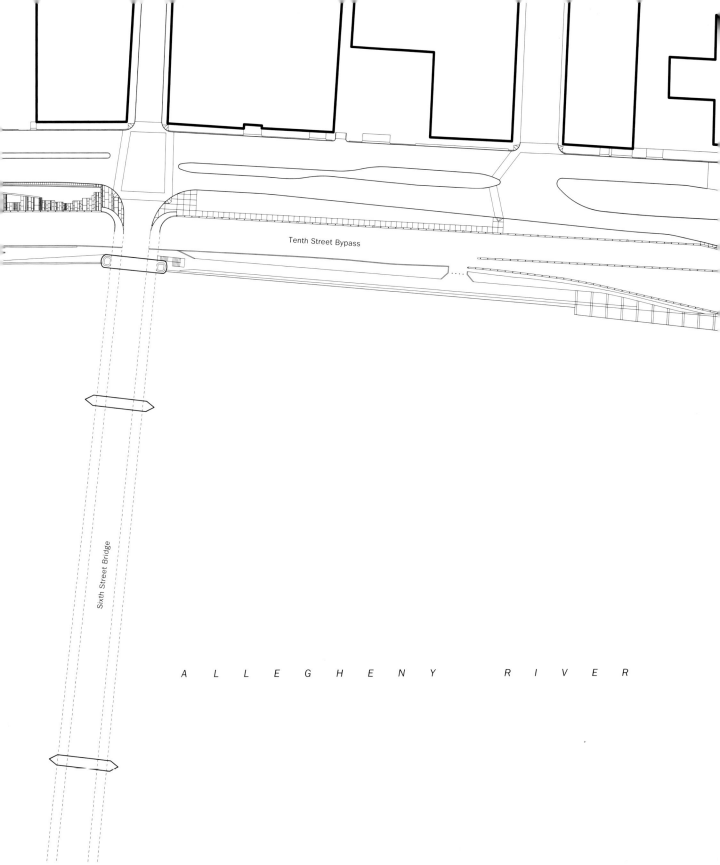

Tenth Street Bypass

Sixth Street Bridge

A L L E G H E N Y   R I V E R

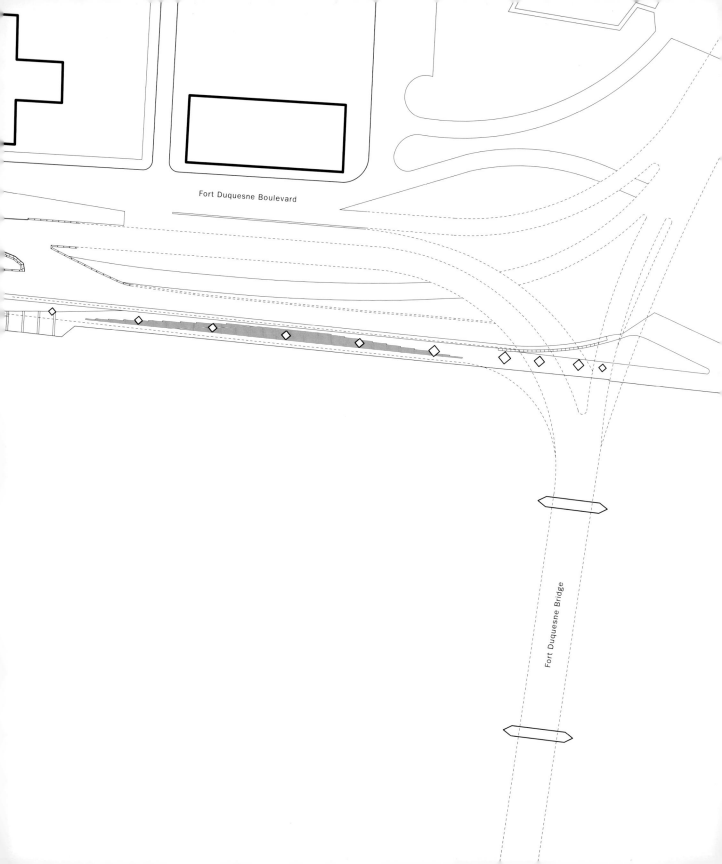

Fort Duquesne Boulevard

Fort Duquesne Bridge

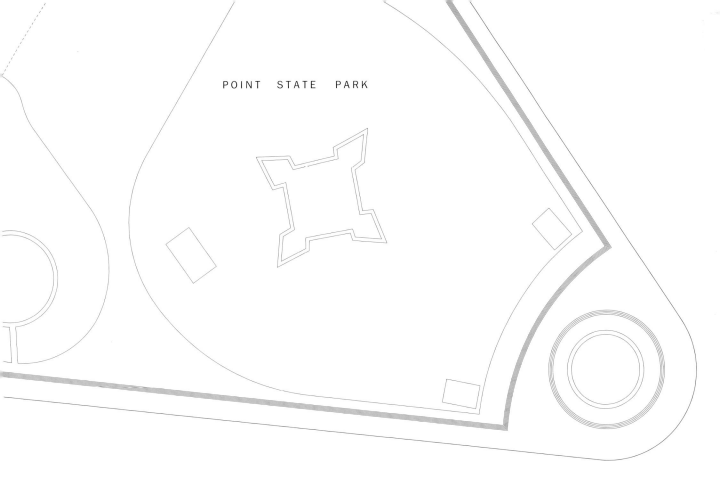

POINT STATE PARK

ALLEGHENY RIVER

Site
Thin Reality

JA: **In February 2003 we held a roundtable discussion about the Allegheny Riverfront Park. The design team, including Michael Van Valkenburgh, Laura Solano, and Matthew Urbanski of MVVA, and artists Ann Hamilton and Michael Mercil, were present, as were three invited critics—Ethan Carr, Erik de Jong, and Gary Hilderbrand—with myself as moderator. In retrospect, two stunningly simplistic conclusions were reached regarding two critical aspects of the project. First, on the potential success of the design scheme: "There is something about the park that makes it more than it is"; and second, on collaboration: allowance for "not knowing" made all the difference. Please explain how these assessments are unexpectedly useful descriptors of the project's design process and the final product, the park itself.**

MVV: There are few smaller American cities that feel more urban than this particular part of Pittsburgh. It has little open space and it presses right up to the river's edge on both sides. It has a palpable intensity about it. I remember going to the site with the design team for the first time. We wandered around the dirty, gritty, noisy, impossibly thin reality of the site's width. There was a six-lane highway on the upper level and a four-lane highway on the lower level with parking. The three bridges were big and ridiculously yellow, and the twenty-five-foot-high concrete seawall felt impossible. The only ways down to the lower-level park site were stairs at the Sixth Street and the Ninth Street bridges. The cubistic on-ramps for the highways were in your face. It was a piece of land that nobody would think twice about. But our client, the Pittsburgh Cultural Trust (PCT), had no other locations for a park. The PCT is an unusual entity. Under the direction of Carol Brown, it has brought forth a remarkable renaissance of small

Existing site conditions in 1994, showing the
topographic division that creates the lower and upper
levels of the park and the highway and seawall

theaters, plazas, and cultural venues in a historic
area of downtown Pittsburgh. The PCT wanted
an exemplary, inventive urban park to help draw
people downtown.

From the beginning the site's limitations—
which a lot of people would have been throttled
by—were taken by us as strange gifts to be reck-
oned with. For example, we agreed that the high
seawall that created an awkward vertical separation on the future park site could be used to gen-
erate a dialectic between the upper and lower park
sections. We never saw the design solution as a
simple unified whole. It's a place that people experience as a series of elongated linear progressions.

When the initial solicitation for the project arrived, it said that we had to work with
an artist woven into our team. My office had
previously had a great experience working with
Martin Puryear on the Vera List Courtyard at the
New School, and then a terrible experience with
another—so I wasn't quite sure how it would go.

Ann Hamilton had just completed a piece in the
Dia Foundation where she covered the floor with
horsehair. There was something about her use of
materials that I felt would connect with our work.
So I tracked her down in Los Angeles, and I had
a sense while speaking with her that she was not
eager—I could hear her thinking, "Maybe, maybe
not." It turns out that her husband, Michael
Mercil, knew of our work and said to her, "If you
ever want to work with a landscape architect on a
project, this is someone that you'll enjoy."

On this project, I learned about the importance of patience when starting a collaboration.
It takes awhile to make new friends, and that's
basically what you're doing when you begin a collaboration. It's important to give that time. Liking
someone else's work doesn't mean that you can
sit down, roll up your sleeves, and know how to
create together. Design is a messy process and not
necessarily a process that should be looked at as
being appealing or pretty moment-to-moment; it's

Aerial view of site with Point State Park in foreground

Catastrophic flood and ice jam on site, January 1996

opposite:

TOP: Crest of 1996 flood and ice jam

BOTTOM: Beached boat and debris post-1996 flood

extra messy in a collaboration. I make a different analogy about design each month, but it's sort of like the difference between a bag of groceries and the finished dinner. The beginning of a design process is like a big bag full of familiar things, such as...what you've done before, what the site is like, what someone wants you to do, all tossed into the big sack. You don't just dump that stuff out and have something beautiful. Design unfolds. If it's good, it takes a long time to figure out—and even longer when collaborating.

Ann Hamilton: One reason the collaboration worked between us is that everyone was willing to suspend their arrival at solutions, resulting in a whole experience, not a stage with art and landscape objects. There was no denial of the site. What enabled the form was that things were never fixed within the design process, allowing for flexibility and willingness to change. It's difficult to say, in the completed park design, "Here's the art

and here's the landscape," and that's one of the project's strengths.

Michael Mercil: This park loves the place it's in, which ironically is a horrible place. It loves those bridges, it loves those bridge piers. It loves being underneath the bridges. You block all the sound from the highways behind you, and the traffic crossing the bridges can be heard—baboom, boom, boom, boom. Those echoings back and forth are part of the aliveness of the place. It contains nature but has no pretense of being a natural landscape. It really feels like where it is—you always know that you are in the city. The toughest part for us as artists was to meet the scale of the city.

One of the particularities of ARP that worked was the level of trust that developed. And the level of trust that our client showed in us. At one point, as the lower level was being finished, I realized that we had done something right—the particularity of that place. When you go there, you feel it.

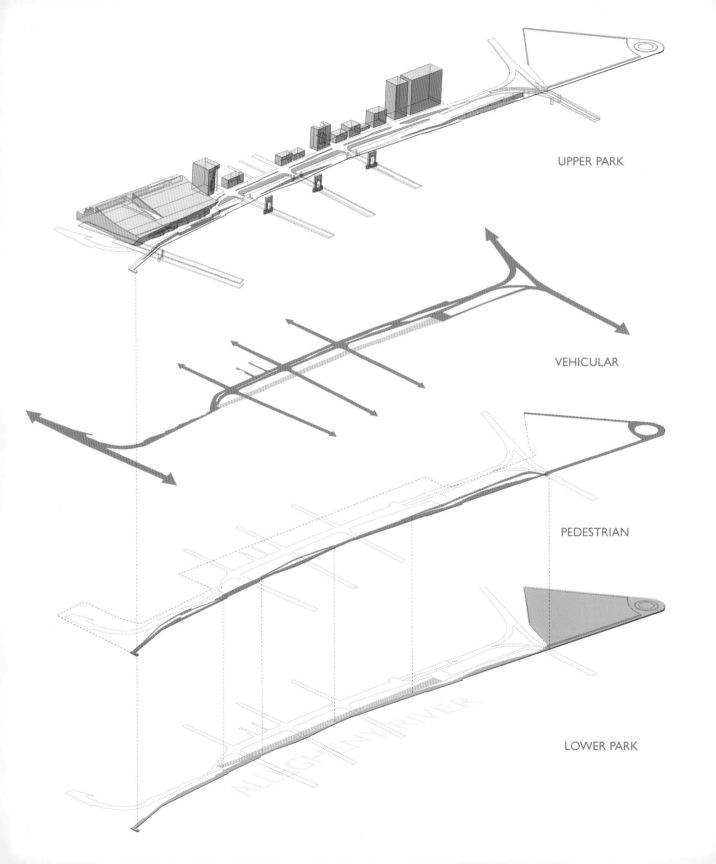

UPPER PARK

VEHICULAR

PEDESTRIAN

LOWER PARK

ALLEGHENY RIVER

It doesn't model itself after any other thing, anything other than what it is. As artists, Ann and my
process is quite elliptical. It's not like someone can
come to us and know what they're going to get.
So these guys had patience for our process.

Laura Solano: Carol Brown had a brilliant urban
vision: to build amenities at the edge of the cultural district, so that people will come in. So before
the district was in good shape, they were working
on a park—a revitalized water's edge—that would
give people a positive experience of the downtown. Carol had to work really hard to convince
others that this was the right thing to do.

Matthew Urbanski: There is a weird paradox in
park design. You talk about wanting to make a
parklike experience, but what does that mean?
When they poll people in Central Park and ask
them what they're looking at, half say, "Other
people." And most of the others are going there to
get away from people. Olmsted wrote about how
a park has to resolve these two completely different programs: one is escape from the crowded city,
one is a democratic plane for social interaction.
How does it do both? They are contradictory. For
instance, we wanted to make a parklike experience
somewhere on the lower level, so when the ramps
taper up, the planting area gets wider. When you
go into the middle of one of the pocket areas on
the upper level, you're in a parklike place; when
you're on the ends, it's more of a plaza experience.
How can you create something that can accom-
modate both in close proximity? It's easy to design
a park to be one or the other—to be the meeting
place where people come together, or to make one
for the Thoreaus of society to get away from the
city and be completely isolated. J. B. Jackson wrote
about these two paradigms in a great essay called
"Jefferson, Thoreau, and Afterwards."

JA: **Your first decisions immediately involved other parties and added significantly to the project's complexity.**

MVV: The upper level contained two three-lane highways with a median and a six-foot-wide sidewalk along the seawall. Our master plan was based on the idea of borrowing the strip of land that was the old median and putting it up next to the seawall. We reworked the grade of the cross slope so it falls slightly toward the city and gives you the kind of view that you want over the water and down to the river. Along the back edge of the new upper park space, stone blocks are set in shallow, open arcs and have earth piled up against them, to create separation from the close-by traffic and to provide root area for trees. By relocating the old traffic median, a six-foot-wide sidewalk became a fifty-foot-wide upper-level park.

MU: We learned quite a bit about the trials and tribulations of traffic engineering—you have to be a pain in the ass to get anything done; otherwise you end up just doing the standard solutions.

LS: The overlapping jurisdictional areas of the project included the river wall on the lower level, owned by the city; four lanes of traffic, owned by the state highway; the bridges, owned by the county; and the park land itself, also owned by the city. The feds ruled the waters; public and private utilities ran through the site. None of these parties wanted us to touch anything. The state highway people didn't want us to put anything that would be in the way of road drainage, like a park. The county didn't want us to even look at the bridges, much less connect anything to them or have the walks go out in front of them. When the ramps were being built, it was still being decided how or if they could be attached to the bridges. On the upper level, the federal and state highway

Sectional relationship of highway infrastructure to the upper and lower levels of the park

opposite:

Park site in the 1930s, prior to seawall construction. Many of the original buildings stand today.

authorities had jurisdiction and had tight regulations about how the traffic lanes could be treated. So we had to keep inserting ourselves into a project we weren't really being paid for. Our client said, "You have to stay in there"; we had to fight the fight. I'd get phone calls like, "We need a turning lane, so we're going to clip off ten feet of the park." I'd reply, "No, and here's why you can't do it."

MU: Our only trump card was, "We're moving this road to make a park…*hello*!" Why did the other parties feel like they had leverage here? Because federal money was being used to move the roads, so it had to be done according to federal rules, they thought.

LS: And we wanted to break the rules. We did our own research on urban roadway standards, which are different than typical highway conditions. We found ways to interpret the rules that worked in favor of the park design.

News about the lower-level park made the project more complicated as we went along. The PCT convinced the city to let it build on this site that it didn't own and didn't know much about. So as the work progressed, we discovered really scary things, such as a huge sewer interceptor line for all of Pittsburgh ran directly beneath the site. There were essentially no soils; the site was filled with coal slag. They built the seawalls and backfilled with slag—not so great for trees. All the bypass water drained into the river and buildings; the park would block its flow. There was the potential for catastrophic ice floes carrying out-of-control barges, and for twenty-foot flood levels inundating the lower-level park. Of the three rivers that come together here, the Allegheny is the slowest, so it carries and deposits a lot of silt that gets churned up during a flood.

Twelve consultants worked with us on a range of issues, from planting soils to river hydrology to ADA issues and civil engineering. In particular,

we collaborated closely with Arup Engineers. They
became another important dimension of our team.
For example, the Army Corps of Engineers was not
interested in us putting support columns for the
lower walkway into the river. They restricted us to
four piers in the water—they didn't care where,
but that's all we got. So Arup designed the cantilever system of precast, inverted T-beams. We placed
all four of our allowed piers at the widest section
of the cantilever, under the Seventh Street Bridge.
Then Arup said, "Bad news, you have to use huge
concrete counterweights to keep the cantilevers
level." Michael said, "Let's express them." Technology has a willfulness on the site. The counterweights provide seating places and formal rhythm
within the randomness of the lower-level plantings. They rest on anchors sixty feet below grade
on bedrock. We couldn't use the ramp itself as a
counterweight because it's hollow—the city asked
us to keep it hollow so they could inspect it. Plus,
if it were solid it would be hard to control the cur-
ing of concrete on the inside.

MM: One of the smart things that MVVA negoti-
ated up front was to take the upper park through
design development at the same time as the lower
park, even though its funding was not in place.
We realized that with the scope and the compli-
cation of all the involved parties—the city, the
state, and the federal government—there was a
risk that the upper park would never be built,
or that it would be given over to the local parks
department. The firm's foresight was crucial; they
made the client understand what would happen
in phase two and helped sell the project to all of
the agencies. Carol Brown had hard questions and
challenges for us, but she was really there for us
in a sense acting as the sixth member of the
design team.

MVV: Allegheny Riverfront Park was really two
projects run end-to-end. The first thing was to
conceive of the park in its totality, as two parts of
a whole.

Scissoring
City, River, Highway

JA: **Let's discuss the park's parti. In particular, describe the scissoring form and the use of specific contextual references.**

MU: Something that we all quickly came to realize was that an awareness of the larger urban form had to be a major force, not just in understanding the site but in determining the formal gesture of the park pieces.

We boiled down the parts of the park and concentrated on the paradigm landscapes that each piece of the park could represent. First, there is the landscape of the highway. As you're driving along the highway near the site there are some pretty amazing ramps, bridges, and abutments that have a kind of modern poetry to them. So there was that infrastructural scale. The river and the floodplain provided a natural model for the landscape on the lower level. Then there is the civic landscape of the cultural district presented on the upper level of the park. By civic, we mean welcoming, comfortable, civilized. It has a material language that is established, even though it's not used in traditional ways. So you have three contextual paradigms: the infrastructural, the natural, and the civic. We strengthened or abstracted each in a layered way. The experience of each along its length has a drawn-out duration. Sensations change incrementally over the length. It's not a cinematic series of images. You get it as you pass through. Carol said, "It's so Zen." It's corny, but in a way that's just what we were trying to do: create something that is calm, has a real duration to it, and you have to walk through it to understand it.

The corollary is that it's hard to come up with a grand idea that is bigger than the force of the highway. But what's in our park works within each of the contexts without trying to bury them. There are some who say, "Why didn't you just

Studying in model how to join the upper- and lower-level parks. MVVA Cambridge office, 1995. Left to right: Michael Van Valkenburgh, Michael Mercil, and Matthew Urbanski

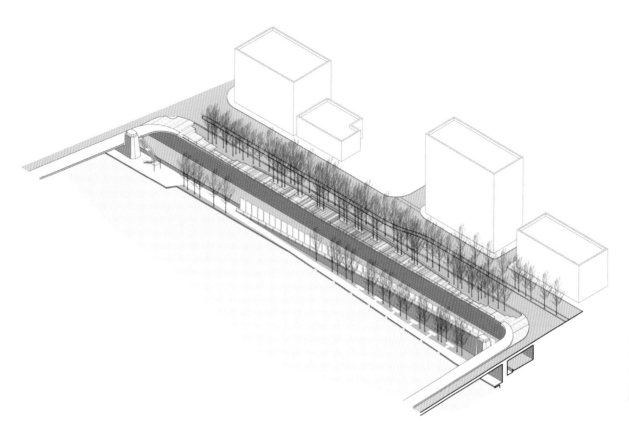

Upper and lower parks are linked by 350-foot-long
ramps that descend symmetrically from the Seventh
Street Bridge. The ramps are an urban-scaled gesture
that enables a dialogue between "urbane" above and
"wild" below.

Park circulation scissors within a narrow slot between city and river

bridge over the highway?" like Boston's Big Dig, and create a totally benign landscape. People long for that. But we were trying to work within the paradigms and meet them on their own scale and toughness. The highway is tough, and the river is tough, too.

MVV: One of the unusual things about the Allegheny project is that it's a linear strip. It's not at all like a traditional park's spatial structure. It's these two half-mile-long things, and the overall effect comes partly from the way the two levels relate to one another and partly from what they make as a linear sequence. It's hard to take pictures of any landscape project that feel at all like the real place feels when you go there, especially at ARP. The place is almost always better than the pictures. When I went to Dan Kiley's Miller Garden for the first time, I was amazed because the photographs of it make it look so compositional, but in fact when you're there it's very fluid.

You see a frame and then you move; it's so much more about fluidity of spaces than about framed views. At Allegheny, because it's so often a one-point perspective, you're always looking straight ahead. The photographs that show the scissoring relationship of the space are the ones that explain the design the best.

MM: The artist Robert Smithson wrote in 1973 that "A park can no long be seen as a 'thing-in-itself,' but rather as a process of ongoing relationships existing in a physical region—the park becomes a 'thing-for-us.'" As artists for ARP, our work does not stand in the park as a "thing-in-itself" but seeks to take its position in ongoing relation to a place made as a "thing-for-us." Because the scissoring scheme inhabits and takes advantage of the edge of the city and river, the place becomes a park and reveals the design team's commitment to material and experimental relationships with the "physical region."

Hypernature
Civic Nature

JA: **When you searched for and pulled in feral fragments from upriver and inoculated the lower level with successional floodplain species, where has this action come from? It comes from something we have lost, both ecologically and culturally. Your exaggerated nature strategy allows small samples to dream of other spaces, other times. Like Robert Smithson's *Non-Sites*, they provide a material reference that is very conscious of its isolation.**

MU: We were worried about trying to make a park on a site that goes under four feet of water every year, and under twenty feet on a regular basis. What could we do? We headed upriver to look around. The old industrial river edges, the steel sheds in low-lying grounds that were used to upload materials from barges, are being recolonized by nature. We saw derelict barges, sunken,

with trees growing out of them. We saw old iron foundry sites with a verdant boundary at just the same level that our park would be. That was it. There were silver maples, river birch, trees only two feet out of the water. We realized that we needed to make a floodplain landscape. But we didn't want to just copy a piece of it. We didn't have room for a floodplain, because the park is a long, thin slice. It doesn't have the breadth or scale of real nature. So we had to do something to compensate. That's where hypernature comes in. It's an exaggerated version of a natural palette. To support the exaggerated density, we used high-tech soils that are well drained, unlike the soil conditions of the real, upriver trees that we saw growing out of swampy marsh.

MVV: Given more space, we could have evoked other spatial qualities of landscape through different kinds of composition. The pastoralism of Olmsted is related to eighteenth-century

Allegheny banks upriver from park site,
September 1994

Reptonian, romantic traditions. Those are compositional ideas that happen in really expansive space, but not here, where it was necessary to pack trees and thicken the experience.

MU: Olmsted wouldn't say "hypernature," of course, but he absolutely says that that's what landscape architecture is. He says that the profession of landscape architecture is to study nature and not just idealize, but to have the viewer see it. Hyper- or exaggerated nature is along this idea. Present it to the viewer so they really get it.

MM: This raises an interesting question. The thing about the picturesque and the pastoral is that it relies spatially on the vista. And the vista is something to be looked at. That's how it's pictorial. It's not something you walk through. You walk to it. You arrive at the vista and then you look out at it. Because we were working in a shrunken space, it dealt more with time than space. The landscape is figured rather than pictured. By figured, I mean giving the sense of the body moving through space in time. When riding down the river, you are enfolded in this valley of trees, but they have no depth. You realize that the trees are these thin slices, like the ramp; they're curtains that give you the appearance of a dense, green city, but really it's just slices of green in a concrete, stone, and wooden place.

As the park matures, especially the trees on the upper level, it's only going to make the contrast between the two levels more apparent. The planting down below is one kind of experience, and up above it's another. In our garden at home is a place that we purposefully keep a mess for my eight-year-old son. It's where wildness is allowed. When he's back there, I don't bother to find out what he's doing. We didn't want to lose that by asserting control there.

Lower-level park defined by exaggerated nature

Flood completely submerges the lower park,
September 2004

opposite:

Boat washed ashore, lower park, September 2004

MVV: To say something about hypernature: we wanted to create a dialectic between the lower and upper levels, between what was "willfully wild" and what was "intentionally urbane." We thought a lot about how the lower level would behave in floods. When you're making a park that a runaway river barge might crash into, you want to allow enough chaos and randomness that if forty or so trees get crushed, some perfect geometric order is not wrecked. So we developed a random tree system on the lower level and used native trees along the banks of the river—things we knew could be broken off by ice floes and regenerate. The hyper part comes from intensifying the density of the planting, creating an exaggeration. Because we had so little space, the experience of a larger landscape came from intensification. As with the Vera List Courtyard, it also was an exaggeration of irregularity. It was much more a monoculture of plants at first, but we ended up planting all of the lower Allegheny Riverfront Park with natives: river birch, silver maple, red maple, cottonwood, red bud.

MU: We always have a strong tendency to dramatically present plants. We like plants and other materials laid against each other to make one appreciate the contrast—a lesson of early twentieth-century montage. For example, the way the trees are cut into the paving in the middle of the upper level, there's no shrubbery to mitigate the scale between the ground plane and the tree. Or the way the trees on the lower level are silhouetted against the depth of that tinted color that Ann and Michael added to the surface of the ramp walls. Or the way the vines are presented on the industrial grating—it's not a vine arbor, it's something else, it's a subconscious thing. Lots of times in planting design you learn to make subtle transitions, but here there's a real intentional contrast, a clean comparison that lets you appreciate both because of the collage quality.

Upper park, civic nature

Lower park, feral nature

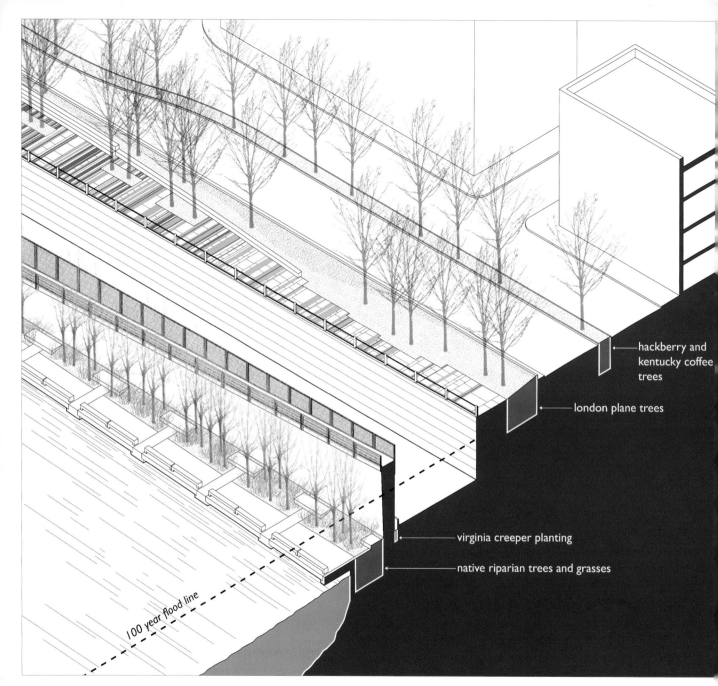

hackberry and
kentucky coffee
trees

london plane trees

virginia creeper planting

native riparian trees and grasses

100 year flood line

Planting diagram

Vegetal and infrastructural layers of the upper and
lower park

LEFT: Large chunks of bluestone individually placed
between cantilevered walkway beams
RIGHT: Use of smaller liner stock trees allows close
spacing of trees between stones

opposite:
Density of new planting stacks up in space to
create instant impact

Similar to the importance of grasping the industrial process of the stonecutting and other materials, being knowledgeable about plant cultivation techniques is critical. The traditional planting detail would not have worked here on the lower level—it's a violent place along the riverside. A tree grown in a nursery looks like the product of an industrial process, or like it went to a finishing school. If you stick those down in a place where we're trying to create hyper-nature, there's going to be an inherent material contradiction. A younger tree adapts better to a site—especially to a challenging site. These trees, container grown, are cheaper, and their root balls are smaller so they fit between the rocks where a bigger root ball of a commercially grown nursery stock wouldn't fit. As a result, I could carry these trees around and arrange them. The trees are close together, so they respond to each other in a way that a nursery doesn't let them—like in nature. The rocks are seats, but also protect the trees

during flood conditions and anchor the root balls. Talk about selecting the right material based on its inherent qualities: the river birch can bend almost in two (during floods) without breaking off, and if it does snap off, it sprouts vigorously. Its root mass will interweave in the boulders. Many landscape architects would have put 450 perfectly matched Bradford pears down there. Knowing the material lets us be smarter crafts-people about the plants.

MVV: One of the hypernature elements is the crust of boulders on top of the tree beds of the lower level. The density of boulders reads as a highly textured surface against the concrete wall and concrete paving. Functionally, the placement and the weight of the boulders help keep root balls in place, prevent soil from scouring, and slow floodwaters. We anticipate they will cause silt deposits too. Remember, at times floodwaters can climb most of the way up the ramp.

On the upper level you'll find something that we don't do often, a monoculture of London plane trees. But we felt that this is such a little outpost of a park, it wanted singularity and intensity. We did use different cultivars so that it's not genetically all exactly the same. In an earlier version, the plane trees were grouped behind the bluestone benches. We realized that the urban street trees needed to engage the bluestone promenade. So the trees were pulled out from the planterlike buffer along the highway edge and moved toward the river.

A big part of the design was stretching the budget. We began this commission in 1994, at the end of a bruising recession. It was publicly bid. Due in part to this, the trees on the lower level were planted really small, which was actually a strategy that had to do with creating density and intensity, but also to save money.

MU: Seasonality is a major interest for all of us. It's hard to deal with that issue in such a small area. The lower park more explicitly tries to deal with that than the upper, because you have the two paradigms where the lower is more of a natural floodplain landscape and the upper is more of a civic landscape. We chose a tree on the upper level that doesn't color up in fall but has a lot of seasonal change throughout the year—a wide, subtle range of distinctions. The bark changes through exfoliation, a quality that's different in the summer than in the winter. On the lower level we tried for more drama. The choice of native floodplain herbs and grasses gives a texture and matrix of planting on the ground plane that's richer and more seasonally nuanced throughout the course of spring, summer, and fall than a lawn or paved surface ever could be. And of course the river birch—the richness of their winter bark quality—was intentional.

LS: I have an alternate take on the seasonality of the upper park. It's about how phenomena act on

Bluestone chunks serve multiple roles by anchoring
and protecting the trees from flood damage, allowing
for informal seating, and providing passive rain basins
for wildlife.

opposite:
Upper park, October 2004

the paving and other materials. The dials are so
turned up on these things that are less apparent
on the lower level. Leaves and snow get trapped
by wind swirling in the bench bowl; rain saturates
the color of the benches; light glistens off of the
pavement; shadows from the rail mark time. The
canvas is very different. The light is so strong in
that part of Pittsburgh that it adds another kind of
seasonality that is much more subtle.

Surface
Trans/Formed Text

JA: **How are materials such as bluestone and concrete—inert, omnipresent in the city— expressed to say something specific about this place?**

AH: The exploration of materials allows the experience of landscape to be felt. We weren't thinking so much about "what focus can we bring here" but more about how we used concrete, stone, or grasses in relation to the bigger landscape.

MVV: I'm interested in how materials make us feel. We explore materials; we go into the field; we go to quarries. We order materials after we have handled them and have a visual on them. We know what we're getting. Much of what bonded our team was understanding that people are walking along and through the park. It wasn't about defining separate spaces but a linear continuum.

So all the things we could do with tinting concrete and plant colors and metals and imprints and railings were about the medium changing as you move along, and the relationship of the materials to the city and to the river. I found some shared sensibilities in our past work and what Ann had done in her past work, and we wanted to join these on site. Materials and space are what convey the bodily experience of a built landscape. In a sense, the materials are the most important thing. Materials in mass makes a space, and it's their surface qualities that qualify the space.

We wanted the upper level to be made from materials that were of Pittsburgh, so that memory of the city would be embedded in the physical materiality of the new park. We decided to use bluestone because of the Pennsylvania tradition. That rankled Carol Brown. She said, "Give me a break; it's too common!" But we all felt it was important. We had to show her that we could use it in a new way, in a transformed condition.

Upper level, bluestone paving

Lower level, reed paving

We wanted to make an homage to bluestone. So we made an intense weaving of bluestone. The stone strip sizes shift dramatically from inches to several feet in width as you walk through the upper park. There's a rhythm under your feet as you move, a kind of morphing and expanding back and forth. Similarly, on the lower-level park the concrete is tectonic and engineered to relate to the river by revealing when the walk is on solid ground and when it is cantilevered over water.

MM: On the upper level, the bluestone promenade was a small thing that became a big thing. For a long time, we imagined the stone pieces set parallel to the flow of the river. Quite late in the game we switched their direction to flow away from the city, over the wall, and perpendicular to the river. The directional movement of the bluestone and its rhythmic shifting of size and shape create a surface sensibility that you can feel through your feet. It was one of those things that seemed so

obvious once we did it. It also changed where the trees were placed and how the benches were set.

MU: The plaza intersections at each end have large pieces of paving stone, up to six-feet-by-six-feet. As you move into the park, there is a visual compression in the stone pattern. In the middle, where the dip and the bowl occur, there are small stone pieces, four or five inches wide. It's not a predictable transition. There's a scalar transition in the paving, a spatial transition in the way that the trees come out and embrace you, a sectional transition with the way the ground dips, and also a kind of acoustical transition as the wall grows out because the land cups you. It's all gradual, not a distinct "plaza A over here, gathering area B over here, and let's connect them with a line." It's all about fluidity and continuity.

LS: The bluestone used here is a metamorphic sandstone found from Pennsylvania to central

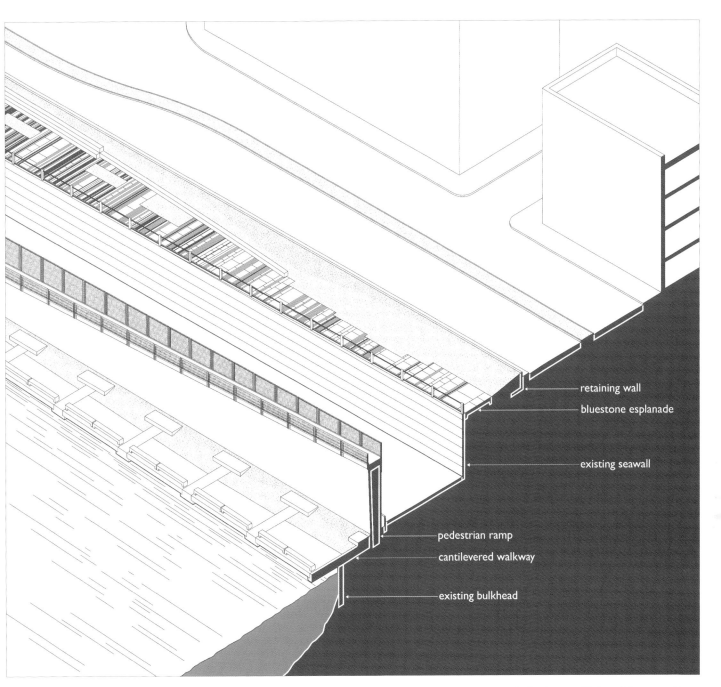

retaining wall

bluestone esplanade

existing seawall

pedestrian ramp

cantilevered walkway

existing bulkhead

Sectional axonometric through the upper and lower
park, cut at the Seventh Street Bridge

overleaf:

Pattern of bluestone paving in the upper park shifts
from six feet wide at public crossings to two inches
wide at center of the park block

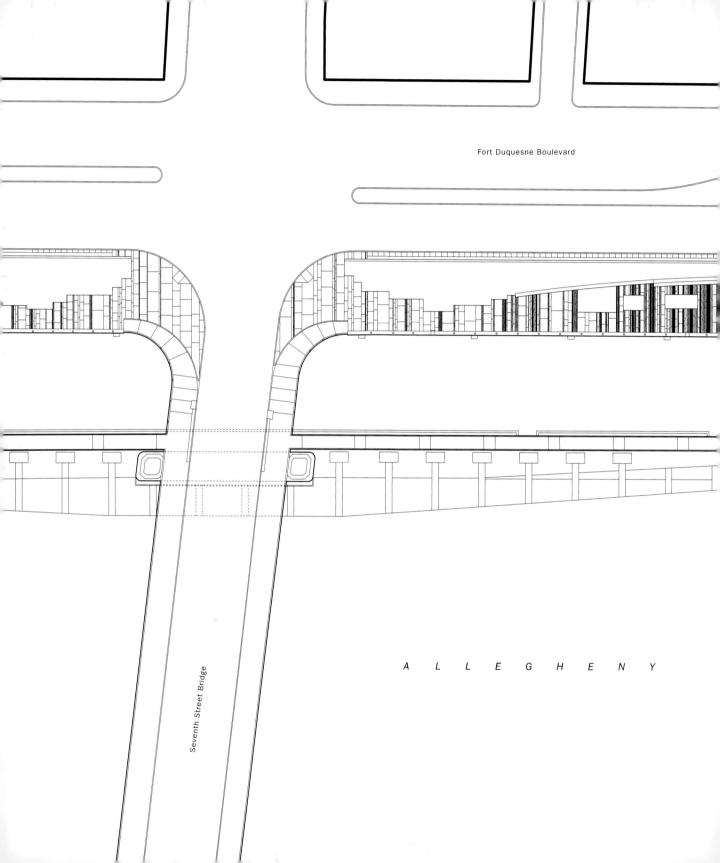

Fort Duquesne Boulevard

Seventh Street Bridge

A L L E G H E N Y

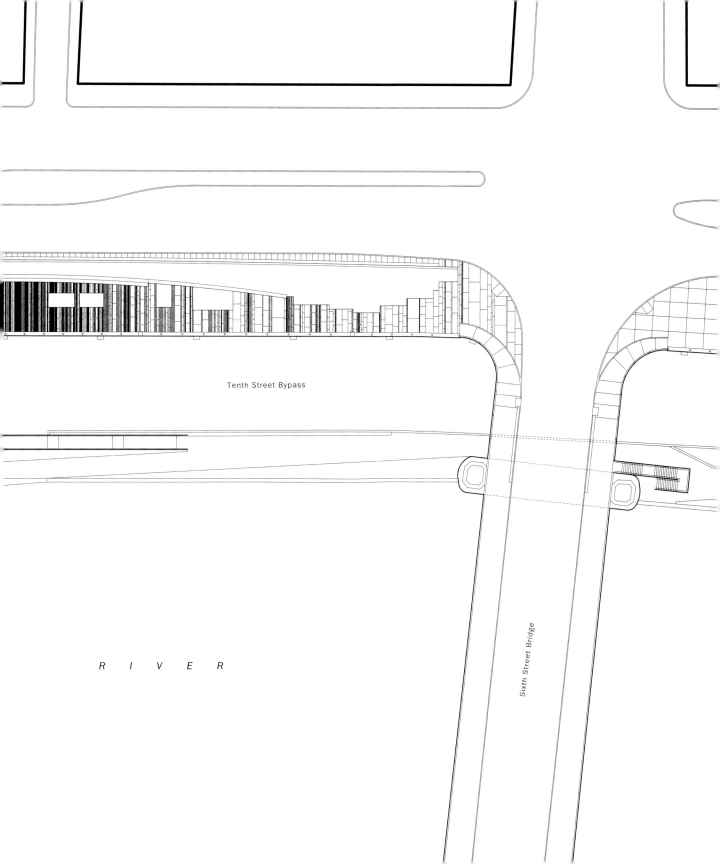

Tenth Street Bypass

R I V E R

Sixth Street Bridge

upstate New York. (As you move north, the stone gets harder and you get different colorations.) We struggled for a while, because the original idea was that we would turn the stone sideways, so that the bedding plane of the sedimentary layers was apparent. On one trip to the quarry, we saw stacks of bluestone that looked beautiful, and we all said, "That's what the paving should look like, we want that rhythm of slices." But we realized that no one with any sense would put sedimentary stone on edge because water would seep in and destroy it. This led to the idea of isolating colors and cleft to texture the pavement. Modulating the size added a rhythm that would let people see a material that was completely familiar to them in a new way.

MU: We told the quarryman that we loved the variation of color. He said, "Everybody else complains that it's not consistent enough and they flame it into blue baloney." He was thrilled. Everyone wants to mill this like boards, but we

wanted to split it along the natural cleft. We respected what he had, and took advantage of an aspect of the stone's inherent materiality.

LS: He did think we were a little crazy for wanting the stone cut into such thin strips. We faced the same issue with the benches. We wanted the benchtop surface to have a natural cleft, but quarry after quarry said no. We had the idea that these big, chunky bluestone pieces of bench could offer another way of seeing what you usually experience in a city. You'd see the bedding plane of the stone if split with a pneumatic splitter, which is hard to do with such big pieces. Finally we found one quarry, Thompkins Quarry, that said, "That's the only way we know how to do it." The same thing happened with the reed paving on the lower level. It took six months of trial and error to figure out how to do it. Everyone I called said, "No, you can't do it, it's crazy." There's a balance of trying to press things in a design process, but at the

opposite:

On the upper level, bluestone pieces run north-south toward the river; the natural cleft surface reminds one of the movement of water and of a boardwalk under foot. The benches are set into the landscape as facts that are functional and sculptural.

same time respecting the inherent qualities of materials.

Both the upper and lower parks were publicly bid and given to the lowest bidder. In both cases we got a contractor who bought into what we were doing. We've found out on a number of other projects that the notion of whoever is doing the building having their head and heart in it as well as their hand is important. For patterning the upper-level bluestone pavement, we specified exactly what would happen across the width (in the east-west direction): ten rows of two-inch-wide pieces, then six rows of this, four rows of that. But along the length, we just gave parameters. We couldn't really control it and we saw the people who were doing the work as having a hand in making it happen. For every two-inch-wide paver, you can make the length anywhere from eighteen inches to three feet long. But here are some rules: you can't line up the joints, the pieces all have to be rectangular, the color has to vary. We weren't

there all the time, so the contractor and subs had to make a lot of decisions.

MU: It's hard to design something that allows that hand of the builder/craftsman to show. The contemporary approach is to eliminate skilled, on-site decisions with specifications. Think about the built works that you admire—often they have evidence of the hands that made them, of choices and changes made on site. Craftsmen have a distinct interpretation; you can feel their attitude. It's almost impossible to design for that, particularly in low-bid situations.

JA: **What is the significance of the reed paving on the lower level?**

MU: Ann and Michael imprinted the concrete walk on the lower level with a wetland reed species that grows along the Allegheny but is illegal to cut. So seeds were collected and we contracted

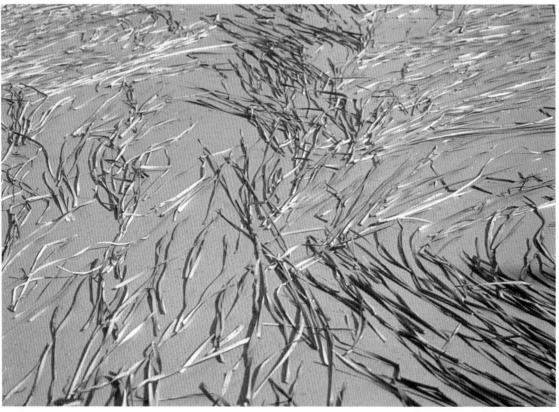

opposite:

TOP: From a rolling deck, Ann Hamilton and
assistants lay the bulrush reeds.
BOTTOM: Bulrush reeds on wet concrete just after
floating the surface

to have the reeds grown in Florida and FedExed to Pittsburgh. Integrity of materials was important— so important that if we couldn't cut local grasses to use, we had to find another means to get them. So although technically they're imported, they belong. These wetland reeds are a similar device as the bluestone on the upper level in terms of referencing a vernacular/natural precedent while also physically implying an exaggerated rhythm and sense of movement.

MM: With the reeds, we were thinking of the way river grasses move just below the surface of the water, especially as the water rises and falls. Ann has always been interested in the information we receive through our feet. The pressed reeds create an illusion that you have come to a different place, even though it's not quiet, or very removed. Reeds are imprinted only over areas that are actually connected to land. If you're on a cantilevered section, it's unmarked, precast concrete. This creates a subtle, repeated threshold that has different elements and parts that are quite distinct from each other. In trying to figure out how to meet the scale of the landscape, we realized the need to keep the gesture open and to keep it large. And to let the material declare its own incident. If you arrange the incidents, then they are experienced in only one way.

LS: To work in the reed texture, Michael and Ann were going to train and work closely with union concrete finishers, but they realized that they had to do it themselves (with assistants) to achieve just the right gesture and feel. Ann kneeled on staging with wheels to lay the reeds, then the concrete finishers came behind and floated the reeds into the top surface. The reeds washed out as they dried.

JA: Is there an intentional dialogue between the choice of bluestone on the upper level and the

Morris Louis, *Broad Turning*, 1958. Acrylic on canvas;
overall: 90 $^9/_{16}$ x 151 $^3/_{16}$ x 1 $^1/_4$ in.
(230.02 x 384.02 x 3.17 cm)

opposite:
Lower-level wildscape grows in front of the earth-
toned wash of the ramp wall

selection of boulders on the lower level? The
refined and the wild—do they communicate?

MM: In the upper and the lower parks, there's
a real play between color and texture, between
concrete, bluestone, and trees. Paintings by Morris
Louis were used to develop a subtle contrast of
colors for the ramp wall coloration. Our idea was
that staining the wall would not just warm it up
but would also prevent water stains from later
becoming visually distracting. We wanted warm
color against the cooler colors, pulled out to the
edge of the water. We couldn't anticipate it, but
the coloration changed the materiality of the wall
and affected the way it related to the trees and the
stone (the bluestone looks very blue because the
coloration is yellowish). This opened up the vertical field as a potential area for manipulation.

Conscious Pragmatism
Ramp, Rail, Scrim, and Movement Strategies

JA: **Speak about the ramp, its vine scrim and sculptural rail. What is the role of this element, beyond the utility of negotiating between the upper and lower levels?**

MU: The ramps come symmetrically down from either side of the Seventh Street Bridge. In retrospect they had to because the site is so narrow and the challenge of the infrastructure comes on so strong. The ramps had to meet the scale of the infrastructure and deal with seventy-five decibels of traffic noise. The scale of the pieces needed to be in the scale of what they're fighting against. A sweet little garden wall wasn't going to do it physically or compositionally. It took a long time to come to the simplest form. We had an open-bottom design for the ramps for a while—something bridgelike. But then we realized that there are already three bridges. And the noise—if the ramps are more like

the seawall, less like the bridges, that helps block noise. Our challenge: 350-foot-long ramps without permitting the profile or the sculptural handrail to be a mindless reflection of the ADA ramp code. The code is so prescriptive that to find any wiggle room for creativity is tough. The ramp is required to have landings on anything over 1:20. But there is a four-inch leeway as to how high the handrail can be in relation to the ramp floor. So by drawing the ramp in section, and then positioning the number of landings, we were able to figure out a rhythm of landings that allowed the handrail to be an average of the slope, to be a straight line instead of echoing the ramp's landings.

LS: The ADA code requires a minimum two-inch-high curb on the ramp and allows for a four-inch variance on the handrail height. For every thirty-foot ramp section, you take up six inches of

ABOVE and OPPOSITE: Steel fabrication built to
withstand ice floes reinforces the concrete
access ramps

grade. If you work out the math, you start with a two-inch high curb at the top of the landing that ends up being six inches high at the bottom of the ramp section. The four-inch difference is within the handrail height tolerance. You get a rippling on the inside while keeping the handrail and curbs on the outside smooth. Here's the trick: the code doesn't say the handrail has to be consistently two-foot, ten inches; it says it has to be within thirty-four and thirty-eight inches. That's why the code-compliant ADA rail can be parallel with the big rail. We did not create stair access between levels at Seventh Street. We took the ADA code to the nth degree—no one can make a shortcut on the stairs, everybody uses the ramp; it is the desirable experience.

MU: When you make a 350-foot-long ramp, that's an opportunity for a bunch of different lines not to look good against each other, or it could be a collection of strong parallel lines. The clean lines directly allow the whole thing to read as a giant, solid wedge. The simplicity of that form—a wedge that is solid on the base—is wonderful.

MM: We worked a long time before the ramps were resolved. Our attitude about the surrounding infrastructure relative to the ramps went back and forth for months and months. We knew the ramps were going to be in the center, but at first we thought they had to be utterly different from the infrastructure. We imagined something light and insectlike. But then we and MVVA came to the same conclusion at the same time: the ramps would be solid. We had to go back to the client and say, "The solution to the central element is to form more concrete." Carol was not happy at first, but then we explained how its solidity would meet the scale of the city.

The ramp itself is a landscape. It creates a relationship between the screen, the vines, and the rail. The rail floats above the ramp, like a sign for

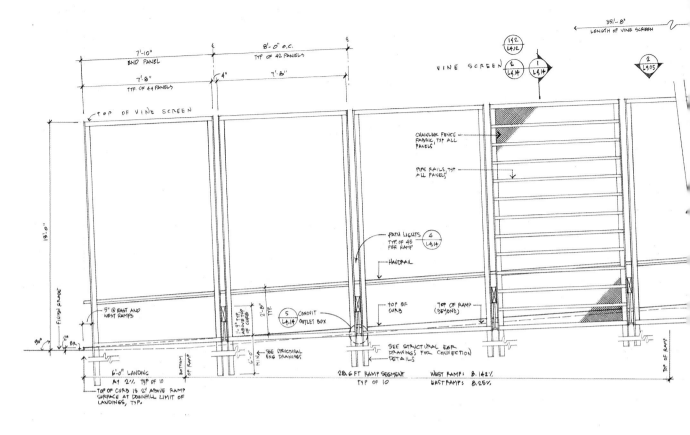

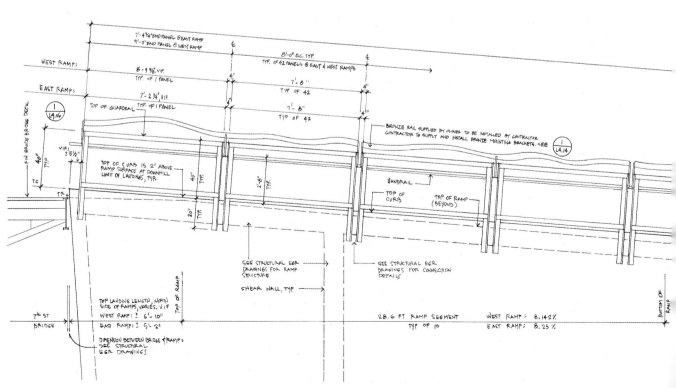

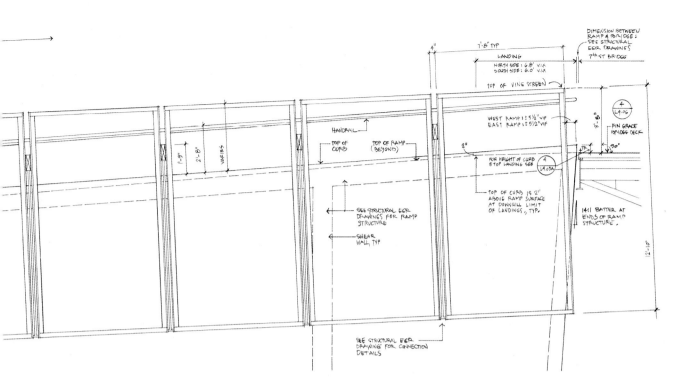

DIMENSION BETWEEN
RAMP & BRIDGE:
SEE STRUCTURAL
EGR DRAWINGS

4"   7'-8" TYP   7TH ST BRIDGE

LANDING
NORTH SIDE : 6.8' V.I.F.
SOUTH SIDE : 6.0' V.I.F.

TOP OF VINE SCREEN

WEST RAMP : ± 5½" VIF
EAST RAMP : ± 5½" VIF

HANDRAIL

TOP OF RAMP
(BEYOND)

4
L4.06

FIN GRADE
BRIDGE DECK

TOP OF
CURB

2"

FOR HEIGHT OF CURB
& TOP LANDING SEE

4
L4.03A

90°

1'-9"   2'-8"   VARIES

TOP OF CURB IS 2"
ABOVE RAMP SURFACE
AT DOWNHILL LIMIT
OF LANDINGS, TYP.

14:1 BATTER AT
ENDS OF RAMP
STRUCTURE.

12'-0"

SEE STRUCTURAL EGR
DRAWINGS FOR RAMP
STRUCTURE

SHEAR
WALL, TYP

SEE STRUCTURAL EGR
DRAWINGS FOR CONNECTION
DETAILS

" PANELS TOTAL

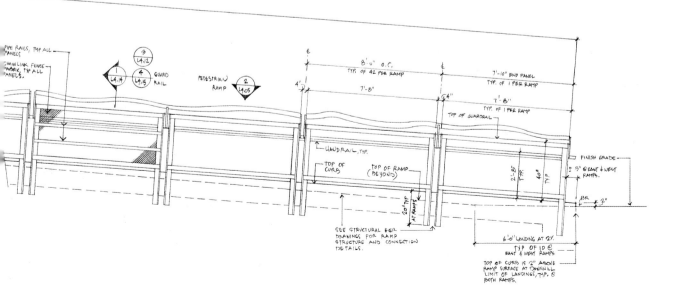

PIPE RAILS, TYP ALL
PANELS

CHAIN LINK FENCE
FABRIC, TYP ALL
PANELS.

3
L4.12

1
L4.14

4
L4.15

GUARD
RAIL

PEDESTRIAN
RAMP

2
L4.05

8'-0" O.C.
TYP. OF 42 PER RAMP

7'-10" END PANEL
TYP. OF 1 PER RAMP

4"   7'-8"

4"   7'-8"
TYP. OF 1 PER RAMP

TOP OF GUARDRAIL

HANDRAIL, TYP.

TOP OF
CURB

TOP OF RAMP
(BEYOND)

2'-8"
TYP.

40"
TYP.

FINISH GRADE

± 5" @ EAST & WEST
RAMPS.

BR   2"

20" TYP
AT RAMPS

SEE STRUCTURAL EGR
DRAWINGS FOR RAMP
STRUCTURE AND CONNECTION
DETAILS

6'-0" LANDING AT 2%
TYP OF 10 @
EAST & WEST RAMPS

TOP OF CURB IS 2" ABOVE
RAMP SURFACE @ DOWNHILL
LIMIT OF LANDINGS, TYP. @
BOTH RAMPS.

Virginia creeper engulfs the highway side of the ramp
structure.

opposite:
Rectangular screens of Virginia creeper float up and
off the back side of the ramps to join the geometric
formality of the city to the less ordered, robust
landscape of the lower park.

a railing without ever quite becoming a railing.
As you move up or down the ramp, the rail lifts a
little bit up into your view. The form of the ramp
extends down to the river, pulls in at the bottom, and then folds back up to the city. It reaches
across the whole landscape. This unfolding is one
means by which for the visitor passage of time
and duration of movement become physically
experienced rather than pictured.

MVV: We always liked that the randomness of the
overall planting was drawn together by the symmetrical ramps and the way that the pair of park
spaces were formed, creating a gentle kind of axial
middle, a strength of slight order.

MU: Along the ramp, creating a visual and acoustical separation between the highway and the
park, the thirteen-foot-high chain-link vine scrim
is planted with Virginia creeper, a fast-growing
and hardy variety. It's too vigorous for some

applications, but perfect for this. Growing as it
is, on the edge of a highway, it needed that
much vigor. The vines climb up from planters
on the highway side. It's the only planting in
the park that is irrigated. Last season they grew
twenty feet.

The vine scrim gets higher as it descends,
so the ramp looks longer when you look up and
shorter when you look down; it's a forced perspective. The scrim is a rectangle, and references
the highway. It almost looks like the back of a
highway sign; its galvanized steel might be found
along a highway. It descends at a slightly less steep
rate than the ramp. Even though it's one of the
long-duration experiences, it changes along the
way. It isn't jumpy; it's a gradual change, sort of
French-inspired, like the subtle, planar grading
over long distances at Vaux. A totally asymmetri-
cal condition; you think of a stair or ramp as a
symmetrical condition, but it's not. It's a balcony
overlooking the river.

LEFT: Artist's photo of branching tree
RIGHT: Handrail modeling

MM: The kind of information that Ann and I brought to the project at the beginning ties closely into the final design of the ramp and rail. At one of the first meetings, we showed a number of images. Joseph Stella's paintings set a visual precedent for us about the basic acceptance of the city. The condition we're dealing with is primarily an urban, built condition. Picasso's cubism provided another visual analogy. We were interested in density, compactness, folded-up space. Fallingwater was not a direct source, but it helped communicate the later moves of the cantilever. Mondrian helped us conceive of how to re-present nature and urban conditions. We looked at a painting by Georgia O'Keefe with a line that moves up and back into the sheet of paper—like looking up the railing. We thought about Hadrian's Tower and a Carl Andre piece with bales of hay horizontally snaking across the field as a way to get at the notion of taking the vertical and laying it down. As we began making early models of the handrail,

the engineers wanted to know how to figure out its twisting form.

MU: We never could draw these. There was just a small bit of space that the rail rotations could move in—it moves around within a space the size of a football. We weren't sure how something 350 feet long only moving within that zone wouldn't look like a zipper or something. But it doesn't. It works within really tight parameters because it's not regular.

MM: The rail is cut into segments, an acknowledgment that the parts never quite make a whole. Sculpturally, we worked with two really wonderful assistants. I went in every day for months, we adjusted the form little by little—add here, take away there, we would flip and turn the piece. It was a process of perceptual measuring. Things I thought I never would do out of basic sculpture class. It was a question of keeping these things

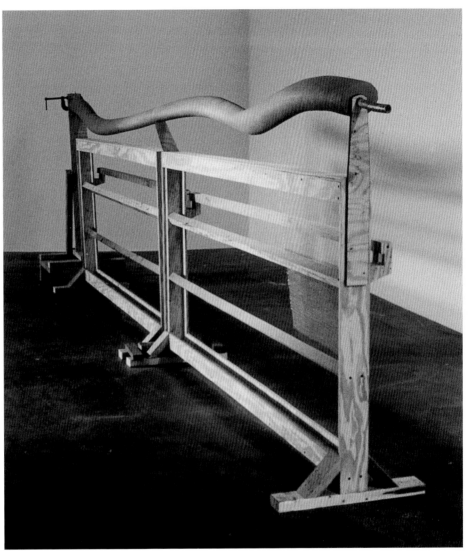

Handrail section, clay and wood mock-up

overleaf:
Ribbonlike forms were modeled at the artists' studio
as four clay sections, each 16 feet long. Each section
was cast in sets of eleven. Individual pieces were
randomly selected on site, then rotated counter clock-
wise or end-to-end to assure visual variety along the
350-foot length of the rail.

Twisting, turning, and hovering above the planar slices of the ramps, the undulating line of the handrail evokes water rolling down the river.

feeling alive. Something would become lumpy or droopy. We asked, "As we spin these, how do they change?"

MU: The railing is bronze. A handrail, you're meant to touch. If you think about your conventional bronze sculpture, it's vertical. It's a man on a horse; you're not supposed to touch. The meaning is very explicit: memorial to the penis. Every piece of this is turned upside down, horizontal. Everyone is meant to touch it. Typical of Ann's work, its meaning is layered, you can't pin it down. One time you'll look at it as a vine, another time it looks like flowing water or a water chain when seen from below. It's less of an object—it takes your eye along it, but then past it too, which is so important for that sense of movement as you look up the ramp.

MM: It's meant to be marked by people, meant to record the human presence. Neither Ann nor I had made anything out of bronze. The handrail was modeled using bent electrical pipe. A Styrofoam core was laid over the pipe, then shaved down and roughly shaped, with clay added on top of that. The four completed sections were duplicated eleven times, then randomly ordered and rotated along a common axis. The individual placement was worked out on site. But the ends always meet at the same place.

I am a fanatic about form, and am much more of a traditional sculptor in that sense than Ann. As we worked on the handrail, the bluestone benches, and the paving textures, there wasn't a distinction about what was the landscape and what was the art—there was an overlap. We share sensitivity about responsiveness to what's there—nothing was a picture or an imitation.

JA: **How does the configuration of the ramps and upper and lower pedestrian spaces respond specifically to the site's constraints?**

Foliage, bark, concrete, bronze, and steel offer constantly changing, complex patterning.

ALLEGHENY RIVER EL.(710.0)

MU: The ramp doesn't double back on itself, like a typical ADA ramp would. That would take up too much room. The ramps are long, thin lines and are battered; the base gets narrower as it gets higher. We had to figure out how to refine it, how to visually lighten the rampway. Because of the battering, as soon as it was built, it lifted up. It sort of disappears; you almost float down into the park. And on the lower level, it creates a sense of generosity, giving a little more room for planting. It takes something that could be dead and gives it a sculptural presence. It's responsive to the human body, responsive to plant life, and its solidity cuts down on traffic noise. We've worked on several waterfront parks. Most waterfronts have one characteristic: they are long and thin, so they dead-end, are potentially monotonous, and have a limited number of entrances. To make a waterfront into a public landscape, you have to offer choices as to how you enter and move through it, for safety's sake and also to alleviate monotony.

In terms of working and inventing from what we had, we realized that between the bridges the tops of the seawall dipped, probably because of some engineering expediency like clearance for trucks on the lower roadway. Those dips became the formal generator for the whole shape of the upper-level park. We could not rebuild that wall—it would have cost millions. We could have added a cap to level it off, but it already had a nice handrail that we restored. Emphasizing the dipping of the top of that wall became another drawn-out subtlety that we played up. The areas behind the dips became shallow bowls, which the upper park amplifies. This raises the importance of understanding the form of what you have on and around a site. You must conduct a form-based site analysis along with your other initial considerations. The site has a form to it, a grain to it, a gesture to it. The master plan (by others) that we began with didn't acknowledge the plasticity of that form and pretended that it was some

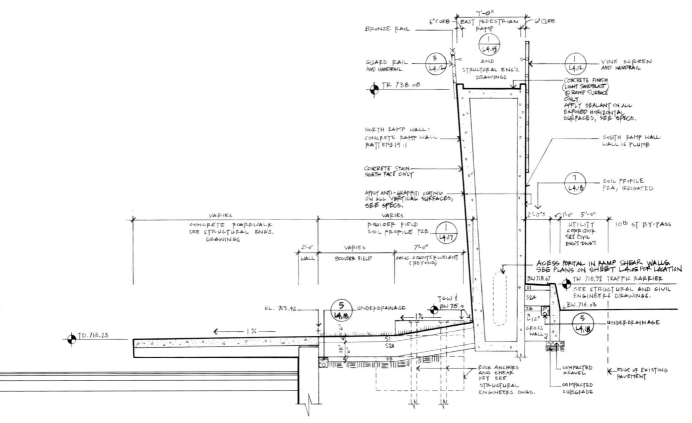

kind of Beaux-Arts, straight and level promenade along the top. So we rethought that aspect, and it became the sculptural beginning. To create the bowls, we raised the level of the back of the upper park, and then elevated the roadways so that they stepped up to meet the raised edge. Instead of growing out of the grade, the stone block benches redescribe and parallel the same dip in the ground plane. The centerline of the benches responds in plan to the dip in section. You feel that space.

LS: There's a two-and-a-half-foot drop from the corners to the center of the upper-level park. You are quite literally in the park. The drop rolls into and then steps back at the ends of the park to create a kind of plaza entrance that is part of the city. To achieve both, the transition is gradual and executed at many scales.

MVV: The combined cross section of the upper- and lower-level park is instructive to look at. The

lower-level walkway had to be fifteen feet wide, as promised by the mayor in a public meeting. This, combined with ADA codes that set the ramp width at five feet, left us with little planting width. That's a tough site to produce a park of significance. That's where Matt's idea for the cantilevered lower walk came from. The main lower-level walk is not parallel to the bulkhead, but is slightly oblique to it. This does two things: first, it lets you have enough room to do plantings; second, you're turned slightly as you're walking down the path, so what's in front of you is the river. It's a subtle shift, but over a great distance it makes a huge difference. It lets you go around the front, riverside of the bridge abutment and look out on the river, rather than being squeezed between the abutment and the wall if the walkway were to go behind the Seventh Street Bridge.

The lower-park walks also slope downward gently, so that when you get out over the water as you pass under the bridge, you're just two feet

Pre-existing subtle cupping of the ground plane
strengthens the volumetric definition of upper level

Lower-level walk shifts outward and pushes downward
to orient away from land and toward water

from the water's surface. We had to cut down the seawall bulkhead to allow the walkway to swing out and around the abutment as low as it does. The concrete benches along the cantilever came late in the design to mark the edge.

MM: Ann and I didn't like the benches at first. We thought the edge should be clean. But it works better with them there. It creates a threshold. And those threshold experiences are really important. We did a lot of mock-ups, and were aware of the differentiation between these benches and the bluestone benches on the upper level.

JA: **There's a significant amount of pedestrian traffic on the bridges. What's the effect of this proximity, of this viewpoint looking down onto both park levels at the same time?**

MVV: The PCT wanted a waterfront park. The site set us up to think about it as a linear experience in

space through time. It's not about views and static conditions but is a park as circulation system, whose success comes out of connectivity.

MM: There are places where you can feel alone, isolated, but the park is very open. There is no place where you're not available to other people's view, even though there are plenty of places for a sense of privacy.

Because we agreed that the park would physically embrace both its natural and urban site conditions, we placed the lower park not just alongside the river but in and over the water's edge. The flow of people, cars, and trucks streaming along the Tenth Street Bypass and the bridges remains integral to the park landscape. The artwork weaves directly into the structure and fabric of the place rather than standing apart as an object or event. Both in space and through time art and park reinforce one another as a singular system of natural and cultural encounters.

Urban Land

Park Complex

JA: **Michael, how has your thinking about parks changed as a result of working on the Allegheny Riverfront Park?**

MVV: Mill Race Park in Columbus, Indiana, was our first major park project, and with the ARP we revisited many of the issues that we faced at Mill Race but in an entirely different physical circumstance. Both had the challenge of severe site flooding, but Pittsburgh was so much more urban. In Pittsburgh we also had added intense infrastructure challenges and responded to a spare budget.

Today Pittsburgh's downtown is on its way back, so different from when we started there a decade ago, and ARP plays a big part in this vigor: It shows how much more livable cities are with parks. It makes me want to know more about the public discourse of the first half of the nineteenth century, in which great thinkers such as Thomas Jefferson and Andrew Jackson Downing were having public conversations and writing essays about the role of parks in the lives of city dwellers in a democratic society. Parks were being discussed in the same conversations along with museums, concert halls, railroads, sanitation, and roadway systems.

For our present landscape architects to reclaim that leading role in society that Olmsted and many others held, as landscape urbanists, landscape architects today need the capacity and the willingness to discuss parks and all urban landscapes on their own terms and for their civic value, and to avoid using the often inappropriate concepts of architecture. They should assert and add to a rich historical dialogue about landscape that needs updating and expanding.

I am heartened about where this dialogue will go, and I see its potential all through the country where, in the last decade, park designs have emerged in places as diverse as Pittsburgh,

Charleston, South Carolina, and New York City. As landscape urbanists, landscape architects are the only design professionals who fully understand the complexity of a park as an urban social organism. But we are picking up this conversation about parks at a very different time in the history of cities in America, a time when people are asking what the ideal city is for a democratic society and what role landscape plays in that vision. Surely this conversation is going on here and there, but not among leading public thinkers, as was the case when the idea of Central Park emerged.

Olmsted's work is occasionally ridiculed today because the world was unable or unwilling to take care of what he gave us. We have seen private entities rebuilding Central Park in the last twenty years. So today's landscape architects must not only reposition parks in the idea of what a great city is, but also be capable of designing and projecting the long-term implications of what it means to effectively care for these landscapes.

I see this understanding of long-term care as a moment of emancipation for landscape architects because the unique inherent quality of landscape is how, as a living medium, it changes over time. It is not that Olmsted and Jackson didn't understand this, rather they understood it so well that they expected that we in the future would have the same commitment to long-term care. They were either wrong or unaware of how many other things would need limited public dollars, once initial park-building investments were made. To succeed, we need to connect how this expensive side of parks, their maintenance as living systems, is also directly related to what people need most from urban parks: their dynamic, unpredictable, changing qualities.

The visceral nature of parks is the opposite of the virtual that so pervades our Information Age. The trees on the lower level in Allegheny are palpably close to you when you are there, and their rough bark and thickness play in extreme contrast to the soothing water sheet of the river nearby. This kind of thing is impossible to photograph, and understandable only when it hits you in the gut as you are standing there. Working in Pittsburgh extended my understanding that the significance of parks is their contribution to the daily life of urban dwellers. They have the potential to unlock imaginations by offering up a million different versions of the kind of physical contrast I just described, bringing us back to Bachelard's idea about psychological immensity and its relationship to the forest. City dwellers don't just want parks; they need them so they can be connected to time and place.

Gallery

Outside the Self

Gary R. Hilderbrand

The Allegheny Riverfront Park of Michael Van Valkenburgh Associates, conceived from the outset with artists Ann Hamilton and Michael Mercil and international engineering firm Arup, proves that a collaborative model of action can work for the making of a public urban landscape. The willingness and skill required to promote shared design responsibility are rare commodities, however, and in Pittsburgh they have resulted in a work of unusual originality and uncommon success. Indeed, while the park exhibits several ingredients that would appear to be attributable to the artists or the engineers or the landscape architects, the project team reports an intense and overlapping collaborative spirit that enables each to claim more than the usual intellectual purchase on both the parts and the whole.

My interest here is in the two-way street of Michael Van Valkenburgh's artist/designer ethos. An artist in his own right, he nonetheless seeks the artistic input of others. He has demonstrated a readiness to collaborate with colleagues and artists in ways that increase the potency of meaning and experience in projects. Among the characteristics that contribute to this collaborative disposition: a confident self-reliance that arises from a deep and practiced love of landscape architecture, and a sensibility rooted in the close study of artists whose own production is shaped by investigation, experimentation, and the careful development of personal conviction within the core of a project's ideas.

Those who have heard Van Valkenburgh talk about his work know of his fondly stated devotion to plant life. Yet while it may seem obvious that a landscape architect professes a love of his medium, the sustained intensity displayed here is far from the usual. Moreover, by the example of his incessant drive toward a more creative application of both conventional horticultural technique and experimental trial and error, Van Valkenburgh has, for over two decades, helped the field return its focus to plants, soil, and climatic effects as an ever-growing source of expressive potential. Rather like the heroic Dan Kiley of a previous generation—whose personal knowledge (and love) of plants has rarely been discussed but was abundantly clear to those who worked with him—Van Valkenburgh turned his affinity for the hedgerows and orchards and groves of agricultural landscapes into an obsession with planted forms and their possibilities for shaping spatial experience. A passion rooted in childhood evolved into a broad, investigative practice. In this case, it also evolved into innovative ways of teaching design with plants to students—and to other teachers and practitioners astute enough to pay attention.

Again, this was far from the usual. Here it is worth recalling the observation made by the iconoclastic James Rose in 1938 that for most landscape architects, knowledge of plants was "a matter of indifference" often dissociated from design. As a reaction to the conventional stance of his Harvard teachers, Rose claimed that landscape design was locked in a kind of esoteric spatial, formal vocabulary—largely inherited from

architects—and sadly bereft of the rich material qualities that plants offered.

Few heard Rose's call, and the long period between the late 1930s and the 1980s did little to change this, especially as landscape professionals pursued the challenges of suburbanization and the environmental movement. But by the late 1980s, Van Valkenburgh's recurring fascinations with color, light, reflection, wetness, frost, growth and habit, and sequential seasonal change would have pleased James Rose and Constantin Brancusi alike. Projects such as Radcliff, Ice Walls, and the Walker Art Museum demonstrated his firm's experiments with water flows, ice accumulation, weathered copper, mirrors, plastics, and hydroponic plant growth, and revealed an appetite for process as a defining aspect of artistic production.

Van Valkenburgh's devotion to the medium extends beyond the material explorations in his landscape works: as a curator, he developed two notable exhibitions based on the work of his modernist predecessors and several of his contemporaries. In doing so, he brought forward a much needed discussion of the spatial and material aspects of historical and contemporary projects. His exhibitions, publications, and gardens reached an expanding audience of students, professional colleagues, and patrons eager to engage in the rising interest in the field of landscape architecture.

The less obvious and more revealing aspect of creative development in the Allegheny Riverfront collaboration is a direct identification with artistic practices that are not typical of professional design offices. That Hamilton's deeply thoughtful and culturally embedded works would coincide with the Allegheny Riverfront's pragmatic demands may not have been preordained. But Van Valkenburgh has always embraced the reach and ambition of driven artists. This inclination to mine a depth of artistic rigor was affirmed in his 1989 publication *Gertrude Jekyll: A Vision of Garden and Wood*, written with Judith Tankard and Carol Doyle Van Valkenburgh. Based on a cache of 2,100 photographic studies by Jekyll of her own garden

at Munstead Wood, the book probed Jekyll's horticultural trials and failings, her attempts to improve documentation methods for experiments in plant growth, her painterly and decorative obsessions, and, most compelling, her strenuous efforts to overcome the limitations of nearsightedness in the drive to perfect spatial and visual pattern and dynamic composition.

In the introductory essay to the book, the authors argued that landscape architects should loosen the proscriptive simplicity of modernist expression and expand their frame of reference, critically, on some significant traditions of garden-making that had long been ignored. On the surface, they sought greater acknowledgment of a place for herbaceous plants and the seasonal flower border in the current garden vocabulary. More broadly, the implication of their discussion, in the context of Jekyll's experiments with color, texture, and bloom sequence, was not a historicist revival of a traditional type—admittedly the typical response to history during the 1980s. Instead, they challenged scholars and practitioners alike to continually reexamine the traditions of art and design as a way of upending a reliance on convention and reengaging plants as a medium in contemporary terms.

The authors also maintained that the typical modernist bias against complexity of color, profuse texture, or even the very presence of flowers, stood in opposition to the values and desires of the wider public culture—in short, people love flowers and they desire to include them in their gardens. While landscape professionals largely ignored flowers, gardeners had never banished them from the vernacular. In this was a clarion message for garden design professionals to get relevant. And the timing of this tour-de-force message was outstanding: it presaged a vast growth in the garden design culture in North America.

Navigating these overlapping motivations—personal agenda merging with frequent assertive charges against the discipline's wider intellectual challenges—produces a character of artistic pursuit both acquisitive and selfless. This latter quality, aimed toward the greater good, propels the artist toward positive collaborative outcomes. The Italian writer Italo Calvino touches poetically on this as he promotes the shared humanist benefits of a work of literature. Writing of myriad unspoken threads of thought that lie beneath the final shaping of words on a page, he alludes to the potent substance of selfless work:

> Think of what it would be to have a work conceived from outside the self, a work that would let us escape the limited perspective of the individual ego, not only to enter into selves like our own but to give speech to the bird perching on the edge of the gutter, to the tree in the spring and the tree in the fall, to stone, to cement, to plastic....

In this context, many of the works of Michael Van Valkenburgh and his colleagues Laura Solano and Matthew Urbanski could fulfill Calvino's goal—conceived from outside the self, escaping the limited perspective of the individual ego, and ultimately giving life to qualities: moods and feelings, the horizon, sunlight, shade, shadow, scent, moisture, even time.

Landscape architecture sometimes operates from the powerful conceit that the concerns of its protagonists are thorough and omnipotent, borne of an ethical charge, determined to solve it all. More often than not, this perspective results in a watered-down, glib kind of problem-solving equation with conventional representational imagery. Countless landscapes are fashioned from this weak position; we encounter them every day. But there is another way, demonstrated ably by the participants of the project at hand. The practice of Michael Van Valkenburgh Associates has built on the particular and individual strengths of the principals, and developed those into a secure and confident base; this in turn enables them to know when and how to build effective partnerships with others.

Great and durable urban places never emerge from one person's idea or vision. No matter how able or motivated a designer or a civic leader may be, the establishment of place occurs through collaborative and evolutionary means. The memorable spaces of Rome's Piazza Navona, or Barcelona's Ramblas, or New York's Central Park, or even Boston Common or Lexington Green, have been transformed through multiple points of view and overlapping time frames. Yet in today's rapid economy of wholesale urban recapture and reuse, the mechanisms of city-building increasingly short-circuit time and build on accelerated cycles of real estate redevelopment or subsidized infrastructure replacement. As we inevitably strive to compress the duration of time in the making of place—as if we have no choice but to do so—collaborations of this kind and caliber offer substantial promise.

Criticism

Ethan Carr and Erik de Jong

The following statements are excerpted from comments made during the Allegheny Riverfront Park roundtable held at the Knowlton School of Architecture.

JA: If the Allegheny Riverfront Park is considered as a potential paradigm for a public park spliced within urban corridors, we must take into account previous models and the new definitions that ARP is offering. In form it is closer to the linear gestures of quays, promenades, and parkways. Does a park by its very definition—take the one established in the United States in part by A. J. Downing and Olmsted in the mid-nineteenth century—offer escape from the ills of the city in expanses of terrain or thin but intensely pastoral landscapes? Even the pocket parks that emerged in the 1960s and urban plazas of the '70s and '80s attempted a certain degree of suspension of urban conditions. In the 1990s, la Villette, Citroen, Candlestick, and other parks offered various guises of modernism's detachment, minimalism's abstraction, and post-modernism's sampling of environmental process-based form, all of which sought "otherness" and none of which provide true registration of the urban context. ARP extends and inhabits its complex surroundings. It is a template of movement and sensation shaped by specific issues of circulation that are recognized with increasing frequency in our cities and urban peripheries.

Ethan Carr: The degree to which we can discuss projects like this as a kind of prototype for approaching urban park systems in new ways is essentially based on creative, limited interventions that serve remnants rather than change vast blocks of the city. These shards, these intricacies of past, great modernist projects of intense urbanization, are very interesting but obviously are fragmented and difficult spaces. I think Michael [Van Valkenburgh] refers to them as complications. Now we talk about turning these complications into assets, which, of course, is a great goal. We're not thinking of them as difficult sites—we're understanding that they potentially make up a park system in other ways.

As a historian interested in talking about things in relation to assumptions about old paradigms, it's clear that park history over the last fifty years has been littered with new prototypes; some of them very successful and very important, some less successful. Historical context is a reality check. So what is notable about the Allegheny Riverfront? There is an idea of knitting together places. It's so simple. If you look at this site, it's not a completed project. It is about guiding a process of transformation—guiding, above all, the plants; this project is about the masterful understanding of woody plants. The results of that kind of understanding happen over time and will determine if Allegheny succeeds or fails. There's also something else that I would describe as a true consultation of the place: the ability to exploit and enhance mechanics that exist on site, to decide what is going to be brought out and transformed despite any perceived difficulties. This is achieved with very solemn rein-

ventions and subtle interventions. It's the opposite of Boston's Big Dig (and I think we need to have an opposite of the Big Dig). The multi-billion dollar job is at the other end of the spectrum from the subtle accretions of seeming minor changes that come together and result in transformation of experience—an emotional transformation. It's economical in every sense of the word, and it allows what we might call the true restoration of a place. Not the attempted replacement of the place, although of course design and preservation or restoration are very closely related activities that share theoretical and methodological origins. The Allegheny Riverfront Park considers how innovative design can be thoughtful restoration. That's the most interesting part of this kind of a project for me, that it is in a very true sense the restoration of the waterfront. It's not wanting to create something that wasn't there. It's attempting through transformation to bring it back, to reinvent it for us instead of replacing it with something that has nothing to do with specifics of time and place.

Erik de Jong: Part of the regeneration of sites is about regional scales and derelict spaces that industry has left. This places landscape architecture into a new context that requires, as in Pittsburgh, degrees of intervention, and results in new typologies. The question of a renewal of typologies within landscape architecture comes from inside the profession as well as from outside. New assignments solicit inventions and influence new concepts of urbanism. For example, bags of sand this past summer along the Seine in the middle of Paris changed that part of the city into a seaside beach landscape, temporarily. It was, perhaps, a bit daunting to see palm trees next to the Seine. But it was a huge success because it drew people into their wish to have a landscape experience in the midst of summer. It showed the attraction of the water in a big city.

There is a change from the concentration on the inward gridding of the cities to an outward landscape perspective. Much of this takes place through transformation of derelict sites. New types of parks can reintroduce or reinterpret the meaning of landscape and nature together with culture and the city. We all know that without a translator we would not be able to speak in other languages. To be able to do that translating is one of the essences of landscape architecture. The literal meaning of translation is "bringing over." Landscape architecture is bringing over concepts and ideas into new forms and functions. It also literally means bringing over plants and stone as embodiments from nature, into a new place. Landscape architecture is the translator as well as the speaker, so the language of landscape architecture is important.

At Allegheny the translation takes place through the organization of space, of which there are three main layers. The space is composed with architectural stone but also the architecture of living materials. There is also the rolling function of art. Really what is happening here is that landscape architecture is a performing art. It is about movement and about life. It takes the elements that exist, like a kind of script, and renews the script and translates it into something new. The performing art of living materials is helped by technology and by the art of Ann Hamilton and Michael Mercil. As in painting, landscape architecture has tried to study and imitate the laws of nature. But it also tries to interpret it. It gives it new form that has meaning. You see at Allegheny landscape architecture as an imitator—not in the sense of copying, but in the sense of study. The study of nature through design and interpretation and translation has been brought into a new context. The making of a park is a divinity between man and landscape. We respect it but also transform it. At the same time it is thoroughly human, especially in the experience of movement—a form of experience that belongs much more to the performing arts than to that of the visual arts. New movement enlightens the Allegheny Riverfront Park and makes it an encounter for nature and landscape and art and landscape art. It is not standard, it is not minimal—this makes it beautiful and exciting. I mean beautiful in the true sense of what the Greek word aesthetics means. The essence of that word is beauty as an experience. That is what a park is for.

Credits

CLIENT
The Pittsburgh Cultural Trust
President
Carol Brown

PARK OWNER
The City of Pittsburgh, PA

LANDSCAPE ARCHITECTS
Michael Van Valkenburgh
Associates, Inc., Cambridge, MA
and New York, NY
Michael Van Valkenburgh
Matthew Urbanski
Laura Solano
Martin Roura
Tim Barner
Tim Mackey
Paul Seck
Gabriel Stadecker
Matthew McMahon
Jason Siebenmorgen
Beka Sturges

ARTISTS
Ann Hamilton
Michael Mercil

LEAD ENGINEERS
Arup, Cambridge, MA

SOIL SCIENTIST
Dr. Phillip J. Craul, Manlius, NY

ACCESSIBILITY CONSULTANTS
Accessibility Development
Associates, Inc., Pittsburgh, PA

BIOENGINEERS
Inter-fluve, Bozeman, MT

GEOTECHNICAL ENGINEERS
GAI Consultants, Inc.,
Monroeville, PA

CONSTRUCTION MANAGER
Oxford Development Company,
Pittsburgh, PA

CONSTRUCTION TEAMS
Lower Level
C&M Contracting, Pittsburgh, PA
Upper Level
Trumbull Corporation,
Pittsburgh, PA

PHOTO CREDITS
All reasonable efforts have been
made to trace the copyright
holders of the visual material
reproduced in this book. The publisher and the Knowlton School of
Architecture apologize to anyone
who has not been reached. Errors
and omissions will be corrected in
future editions.

All images courtesy of Michael
Van Valkenburgh Associates
except as follows:

Ron Bowen: 17 left and right, 23;
Carolyn Brown: 18, 19; Elizabeth
Fellicella: 14 bottom; © Susan
Gilmore/Esto: 22; Clyde Hare:
8 far right; Alex S. Maclean: 37;
Ed Massery: 46–47, 48, 54, 88,
90, 94, 99, 112–13, 139, 144–45,
153; Charles Mayer: 25; Sam
McMahon: 9 right, 60; Michael
Mercil and Ann Hamilton: 84
top and bottom, 85, 100 left and
right, 102–103; Annie O'Neill: 9
left, 10, 43, 45 right, 55, 56, 59,
61, 63, 65, 69, 70, 71, 75, 82,
87, 89, 104, 105, 108, 111, 114,
121–22, 123, 126, 129, 131, 134,
136–37, 140, 143, 147; Pittsburgh
Cultural Trust: 8 far left; Jerry
Speier: 20; Paul Warchol: 21 top
and bottom; Alan Ward: 13 all

Bibliography

"Allegheny Riverfront Park Lower Level." *Land Forum*, Summer 2000, 70–73.

Barnes, Tom. "The Trees of Life for Downtown." *Pittsburgh Post Gazette*, December 5, 1995.

Barreto, Ricardo. "The Art of Universal Design." *Public Art Review*, Fall 2000, 41–43.

Block, Dave. "Compost Plays Role in Riverfront Restoration." *BioCycle*, August 1999, 26–28.

Burger, K., Elliott, S., and Hasch, M. "Park Survives First Dousing." *Pittsburgh Tribune Review*, January 26, 1999.

Craig, John G., Jr. "Getting Better All the Time." *Pittsburgh Post Gazette*, February 7, 1999.

Dawes, T., Fitzgerald, C., and Hodkinson, G. "Allegheny Riverfront Park." *ARUP Journal*, March 1999, 22–24.

Dunlap, David W. "A Chip Off the Old Park; A 1.9-Acre Gem Is to Open Today Downtown." *The New York Times*, September 30, 2004.

Freeman, Allen. "Going to the Edge." *Landscape Architecture*, July 2003, 86–91, 106–07.

Gutnick, Todd. "Decades-Old Vision of Riverfront Park a Reality." *Pittsburgh Tribune Review*, December 1, 1998.

Lott, Ethan. "Trust Hopes Riverfront Park Will Enhance Cultural District." *Pittsburgh Tribune Review*, December 11, 1995.

Lowry, Patricia. "Park Utilizes Native Amenities." *Pittsburgh Post Gazette*, November 30, 1998.

———. "Urban Revitalizer." *Metropolis*, January 2002, 66–67.

May, Mike. "Park 'n' Walk." *Pittsburgh Magazine*, August 1999, 46.

Miller, Donald. "Proposed Riverfront Park a Vision in Green." *Pittsburgh Post Gazette*, December 9, 1995.

"A New Park for Pittsburgh." *Pittsburgh Post Gazette*, December 6, 1995.

Nobel, Philip. "Let It Be." *Metropolis*, October 2004.

"Part Way to a Park." *Pittsburgh Post Gazette*, December 5, 1998.

Pearson, Clifford A. "Allegheny Riverfront Park, Pittsburgh." *Architectural Record*, March 2000, 103–06.

"Progressive Architecture Awards." *Architecture*, January 1997, 92–93.

Raver, Anne. "Landscape; The Call of the Primordial." *The New York Times*, January 6, 2005.

Richardson, Tim. "International Design: Michael Van Valkenburgh." *Gardens Illustrated*, February 2005, 91–95.

Shearing, Graham. "Architect, Artist Have Plans for Riverfront." *Pittsburgh Tribune Review*, December 10, 1995.

Shearing, Graham. "A Preoccupation with the Real." *Pittsburgh Tribune Review*, August 28, 1999.

"The River Runs by It." *Pittsburgh Post Gazette*, December 14, 1998.

Biographies

JANE AMIDON is a landscape designer, critic, and lecturer currently teaching in the Landscape Section of the Knowlton School of Architecture. Her published work includes *Dan Kiley: America's Master Landscape Architect*, *Radical Landscapes*, and *Moving Horizons: The Landscape Architecture of Kathryn Gustafson and Partners*. Recent presentations include discussions of modern and contemporary landscape architecture at the Netherlands Architecture Institute, the Royal Institute of British Architecture, and the Wexner Art Center.

GARY R. HILDERBRAND is Principal of Reed Hilderbrand Associates, Inc. and is Adjunct Associate Professor of Landscape Architecture at the Harvard Design School, where he has taught seminars, design studios, and required courses in the use of plants as a design medium since 1989. His publications include essays in numerous books and journals and he has authored two monographs, *Making a Landscape of Continuity: The Practice of Innocenti & Webel* and *The Miller Garden: Icon of Modernism*. He is a fellow of ASLA and of the American Academy in Rome.

ETHAN CARR is a professor on the faculty of the University of Massachusetts where he teaches courses in landscape history, landscape architectural theory, historic preservation, and design studios. He has worked extensively with the National Park Service as an historical landscape architect and is the author of *Wilderness by Design: Landscape Architecture and the National Park Service*, which received an ASLA award for research. He holds a master's degree in Art History from Columbia University and a master's degree in Landscape Architecture from Harvard University.

ERIC DE JONG is a professor at the Garden History and Landscape Studies Program at the Bard Graduate Center in New York. He is a leading expert on European garden art and landscape architecture and has held fellowships at Harvard University, Dumbarton Oaks, and the Netherlands Institute for Advanced Studies. He holds the Extraordinary Clusius Chair in the History of Garden and Landscape Architecture at the University of Leiden, the Netherlands. His numerous publications include *Nature and Art: Dutch Gardens and Landscape Architecture, 1650–1740*. He also works as a landscape critic, an exhibition maker, and advises on landscape design and restoration projects.